A GROUSE HUNTER'S ALMANAC

A GROUSE HUNTER'S ALMANAC

The Other Kind of Hunting

MARK PARMAN

THE UNIVERSITY OF WISCONSIN PRESS

The University of Wisconsin Press
1930 Monroe Street, 3rd Floor
Madison, Wisconsin 53711-2059
uwpress.wisc.edu

3 Henrietta Street
London WCE 8LU, England
eurospanbookstore.com

Printed in the United States of America

This book may be available in a digital edition.

The Library of Congress has cataloged the hardcover edition as follows:
Parman, Mark.
A grouse hunter's almanac: the other kind of hunting / Mark Parman.
p.   cm.
Includes bibliographical references.
ISBN 978-0-299-24920-5 (cloth: alk. paper)
1. Grouse shooting—Wisconsin—Anecdotes.   I. Title.
SK325.G7P27   2010
799.2´463—dc22
2010012963

ISBN 978-0-299-24924-3 (pbk.: alk. paper)

"Ox" and "Grouse Weather" were originally published in much different versions
in the Ruffed Grouse Society magazine.

Contents

Contents

Contents

Preface to the 2017 Edition

When I wrote the preface for the first edition of *A Grouse Hunter's Almanac* eight years ago, we had just lost our two bird dogs, Ox and Gunnar, the central characters of my book. The preface was the last thing I wrote for the book, and maybe the hardest. The act of writing it drove home what we had lost.

In that preface, I also briefly mentioned our new English setter pup, Fergus, who we had just picked up in northern Wisconsin. He is now eight years old (see "Counting in Dogs"), and a few years later, we added another setter, Jenkins, to our pack. We sometimes refer to Jenkins as Baby, even though he is now five. They are the subjects, perhaps, of a future book.

I, too, have added eight years to my tally, and although I may not be as spry as I was when writing the book, my desire to hunt burns as intensely as it did back then. To compensate for my aging, I bought another Browning Superlight Feather (see "Gun Lust"), this one a 20-gauge, which weighs almost a pound less than the 12-gauge version. I also bought an old 20-gauge Ithaca 37 Ultra Featherlight, which weighs even less than the Browning, and then attached a sling to it for long rambles through the woods. My brother returned my old battered Valmet—my first real grouse gun—and its almost eight pounds now feel like an anvil, a gun so heavy I cannot believe I ever lugged it up and down hills and through the rugged cover of the grouse woods. I was a different man back then. My older brother finally wised up, too, and bought a lighter shotgun.

Other matters I wrote of in the first edition have changed as well. I no longer hunt out at Paul's. His brother built on the far side of the property, and it now feels too settled and hemmed in for a proper hunt, but I found another cover near there that has been every bit as good as Paul's. There is no shortage of public grouse and woodcock cover in northern Wisconsin, and may it always be that way. Some of my other coverts have aged beyond holding birds, the popples maturing and thinning. A few places have been logged, and I am waiting for them to age, like a good sharp cheddar cheese.

On the other hand, many of the things I wrote of eight years ago have remained a constant in my life. I'm still hunting many of the coverts described herein, even though some may not be as productive as they once were. Their familiar geography I treat like an old friend, visiting on occasion whether or not they deserve it.

The grouse opener is typically the third Saturday in September, often a day with a summerlike feel, and the woodcock opener follows the next weekend. Grouse numbers are still cycling inexplicably up and down, and if you're reading this book in a year ending in seven, eight, or nine, chances are the cycle is up in the Midwest, and hunters are seeing good numbers of birds out in the woods here.

I still occasionally get good and lost ("Getting Lost, Staying Lost"), and the Friday before gun deer season ("Black Friday") lives on as one less day to hunt grouse. Climate change and its effect on habitat ("Like Trees, Walking") concerns me more today than it did eight years ago, and I'm always hoping to get one more point, one more shot at a bird at the tail end of the day ("The Mythical Bird"). Grouse hunting, thankfully, remains deceptively and beautifully simple ("How to Hunt Grouse")—may I never overcomplicate it.

Most importantly, I hope my love for grouse hunting never wanes—my desire to pull on my boots, pick up my shotgun, and trail along behind my dogs through the October and November woods.

Introduction

"There are two kinds of hunting: ordinary hunting, and ruffed-grouse hunting," wrote Aldo Leopold in *A Sand County Almanac*. Leopold understood grouse hunting's allure and its extraordinary qualities, particularly in the month of October, claiming that "the other months were constituted mainly as a fitting interlude between Octobers." I get the feeling that despite his many responsibilities, Leopold spent as much of the tenth month as possible up at his Sauk County farm, gun in hand, meandering along behind his pointing dog, hoping for a shot or two and yet still satisfied to come in at the end of the day without one. There isn't a much better way to spend an October day in Wisconsin.

The following essays focus on this other kind of hunting—a simpler and older sort of hunting in which hunters both respect and kill the very thing they so enjoy. The Spanish philosopher José Ortega y Gasset wrote that hunters do not hunt for the kill, but rather they kill in order to have hunted. Hunters, according to him, do not go into the field to steep or rough places of difficult footing just for the exercise or to get a bit of fresh air. In the end hunters kill. We are "death dealers." My hands get bloody, but I refuse to speak euphemistically of what hunters do and call killing "harvesting," as if grouse were apples or tomatoes. I have held grouse as their last life blood shuttered through their warm bodies and watched as dying birds beat their wings in the duff and leaves under a popple stand, one final flurry before their deaths. It's a sobering act to take the life of a bird, and holding one in hand I wish often there were such a thing as shoot and release. That, however, is not the way of the natural world.

In the ordinary hunting of this century, many hunters go afield to kill and return home disappointed without something to show for their efforts. Today the goal often is to dominate nature, unlike Leopold's purpose, which was to participate in nature. Hunters talk about "crushing," "smacking," or "smoking" birds, as if the hunt were a contest scored between the hunter and the hunted. Deer hunters have a saying—"If it's brown, it's down"—and it's small wonder that many among Wisconsin's nonhunting populace fear walking in the woods during the nine-day gun deer hunt. In this annual Wisconsin tradition, over six hundred thousand hunters take to the woods, many hoping to bag the biggest buck of their lives. Families, bars, churches, and workplaces hold big buck contests, and any hunter can compare buck racks with the Boone and Crockett scoring system. In fact, hunters poring over glossy deer-hunting magazines often react remarkably and disturbingly like men gaping at pornography. A friend refers to deer hunting magazines as horn porn, even though technically deer have antlers, not horns. Fortunately, record books for grouse don't exist, so grouse hunters aren't tempted to measure tail feathers or spurs to figure out who shot the biggest bird, although competitive hunters can fall into a numbers game, tallying up and comparing who shot the most birds.

Unlike gun deer hunting, which is a social affair and sometimes the only time of the year when many hunters get out into the field, grouse hunting, for me, is mostly a solitary pursuit. Occasionally I hunt with a friend or my brother, and more often with my wife, but usually it's just me in the woods, following the tinkling of the dog's bell. Like Leopold, I follow the dog through the woods since the dog knows where the grouse are better than I do. A steel bell ringing in the woods is a conspicuous sound, a man-made sound in the midst of much older sounds: the wind high up in the aspen, the creak of an old maple, the honking of Canada geese high overhead, or the wheezing of a fleeing deer.

In ordinary hunting, the hunter often relies on technology to gain advantage over the quarry. Sporting goods stores offer and sell hunters all kinds of gadgets: scent-free clothing, bait, global positioning system (GPS) units, walkie-talkies, laser sights, and all-terrain vehicles (ATVs). Beating nature becomes more important than how one plays the game, and the desire to buy the latest technology drives sales in Wisconsin's billion-dollar hunting industry. For grouse hunters, a comfortable yet tough pair of boots might be the most important gear, or maybe thorn-resistant pants, although a compass comes in handy in big woods. There's not much a bird hunter needs out of a typical Cabela's catalog, but our needs often get confused with our wants.

Grouse hunting hasn't changed much in the fifty years since *A Sand County Almanac* was published. It is pretty much the same now as it was one hundred years ago, when loggers razed the virgin white pine covering the northern half of the state. When aspen regenerated in many of the massive clear-cuts the loggers left behind, the state most likely held more birds than it ever had, and that was a good time to be a grouse hunter. Like a century ago, grouse hunting is still a matter of a bird, a dog, a gun, and cover that holds birds—plus the hunter that binds all together in a yearly ritual.

In our postnuclear information age, grouse hunting seems a quaint, old-fashioned pursuit, like making firewood or hiving bees, and I often wonder if the younger generation will continue the tradition or trade it for a video game that simulates the experience indoors. Grouse hunting seems connected to our distant past, the one peering out at me from old black and white photos at the courthouse and the county historical society, and it's difficult to project its future, particularly when much of the younger generation doesn't seem all that interested in walking a couple of miles over rough country just to get a shot at a bird. That wiry man perched on top of a just felled white pine or the two sawyers pulling the crosscut saw—they would understand grouse hunting. We can only hope a portion of the younger generation will understand it someday as well, and in these days of climate change and shrinking habitat, I pray they get the chance to do so if they so choose.

Sometimes I do not know what to say about grouse hunting to friends and colleagues whose days are spent mostly in man-made environments. How do I describe the thrill of a dog going on point, smelling, to me, an undetectable thread of scent? I trust there is a bird lying somewhere in front of the dog, and my nerves tingle and my palms sweat as I wade in for the electrical jolt of the flush. How do I articulate all of the cover and terrain I've walked through, that particular view down the New Wood River framed by three massive white pine trees? How to express that feeling of a warm bird in hand, the satisfaction of a perfect point and a well-placed shot? How to explain the pull of a matchless October afternoon when the aspen leaves are sifting down like gold coins from heaven?

The essays that follow, starting in late summer and ending as the snow falls in early winter, attempt to do so. My life would feel so empty without the October woods, a dog working ahead and a shotgun cradled in my arms. Like Leopold, I am also one who cannot live without wild things: a stand of white birch against an autumn blue sky, wolf tracks down a logging road, a porcupine-gnawed antler. Things I experience often but seldom explain. Things I experience often that are so hard to explain.

EARLY SEASON

Some August Day

SOME AUGUST DAY, usually late in the month, the jet stream buckles and bends south, and cold Canadian air pours down into Wisconsin, displacing the thick air that has stagnated over the area for much of the summer. Some years this cold might not arrive until September, but every year it comes. I think about starting a small fire in the woodstove, but right now the cool feels bracing, a relief. Summer will make a comeback, the warm air pushing back the dense, cool air to the north. Surely the heat and humidity will return and September will again be a time of cold beer and barbeques, but the chill reminds me of what's to come.

Already the sumacs up the hill are blood red, burning with color. A few sentinel maples to the east of our house and some down in the valley have also reddened and yellowed. Asters bloom in the ditches, and our tomatoes have finally ripened. Daylight is noticeably shorter as the sun slides to the south, angling in our windows more obliquely and with lessening strength each passing day.

My dogs sense the change too. When the temperature climbs to 90 degrees or higher, heat waves shimmering above the asphalt, they move deliberately, seeking the shade at every opportunity, and they know where all the buckets of water are placed around the yard. Some days they don't even seem to want to go on their daily walk, but I'd probably feel the same way if I wore a fur coat and could only sweat through my tongue.

As summer creeps toward autumn, the first cool evening arrives, stirring me to pull my tattered Filson vest out of the front closet. Like the smell of gunpowder, the musty smell of my old vest evokes past hunts in past places. A wave of Proustian memories rolls through my mind, the dank, waxed cotton smell drawing sights and sounds up out of the black well of my subconscious. My clearest memory is of one of the first days I wore the vest, an early September morning before the season had begun. In the cover we walked stood a brilliant maple tree looking as if it were on fire, like the burning bush of Moses, and my vest always reminds me of that tree on that clear day: a few of the leaves scattered in the grass about the trunk, red on green, me in my shiny crisp vest, the waxed cotton still stiff as cardboard, the dog young, dancing at the foot of the tree, whining to keep moving on.

Many years later the dancing dog was gone, but I still had the vest, the left shoulder black and shiny from the autumns of my shotgun resting and bumping there. One of the front buttons was dangling precariously and would not last the season unless resewn. My boots looked like they needed oiling, and I really had to buy a new blaze orange hat as the old one's color had faded to dull pumpkin.

Rummaging in the closet, I found the whistle and Swiss bell and rang it ever so softly, one quiet clank. Ox popped up off the floor out of a deep sleep and bolted over to the closet, skidding into me across the maple boards. He was ready, just as if he had an on/off switch. I walked out onto the screened porch, bell in hand, and Ox followed, nudging the hand holding the bell and nibbling my wrist with his little front teeth. The sun had dropped below the neighbor's roofline, the sky turning from deep blue to purple. Already the waxing moon had climbed into the darkening eastern sky. It felt as though there could be a touch of frost in the morning.

I walked back into the house, closing the door to contain the heat in the house. "Tomorrow morning, Oxie. Tomorrow morning," I promised. After I stashed the vest and bell back in the closet, he slumped over to his pad, plopped down, and curled head to tail, pouting. He couldn't see past the disappointment of the moment, but I knew what the morning would bring.

No delicate frost glazed the lawn overnight, the temperature merely dipping to just below 40, but it was plenty cool for us to get into the woods before the sun climbed too high in the sky. That morning felt right. In the twenty-first century, Wisconsin law states that we can only grouse hunt in autumn in the days prescribed by the Department of Natural Resources (DNR), although a century ago, before we developed a conservation ethic, hunters hunted year-round if they wished—spring, summer, fall, winter. Today we do most of our hunting in the fall, spring turkey hunting a notable exception. Game animals don't give birth in fall, and the young of the year have matured. The days are cooler, making it easier to preserve meat taken, but it's more than that. For me, it feels right to hunt in fall, the time of harvest, although I hesitate to use that verb with game, as though a grouse or woodcock is just a broccoli stalk with wings. Something deep inside urges me to build up a store of meat for the coming winter months. Despite supermarkets that provide us with meat from people and places we know not, I'm drawn to the woods to do my own killing. If nothing else, it's a more honest way of eating flesh and blood.

And so we went out the next morning. The law and the calendar said we could not hunt yet, so my shotgun remained at home in the closet, but I gathered my vest, my old boots, the whistle, and the bell. I rang it once, and Ox slid open his droopy eyes. Another ring and he launched off his pad and bolted to my side, nibbling my wrist with his front teeth, his way of grabbing hold of my hand.

The first time out, we went to the same spot every year, a friend's land bordering the county forest. A narrow trout stream runs just north of his land through the county forest, and tag alders (*Alnus rugosa*) border the creek. It was down by the water that we would most likely find birds. That the dog knew exactly what we were doing once again astounded me, but this wasn't always the case. When he was younger, these early morning jaunts were serious training sessions, dry runs before the season began in earnest.

The land was achingly familiar. I shot Gunnar's first grouse here, and we still have the tail feathers of this bird framed and on the wall. I fired at the bird twice, and after the second shot Susan and I stood there arguing about whether or not I had hit it. I maintained that I had missed it; she said she saw it fall. While we argued, Gunnar approached us sheepishly with the bird in his mouth, his eyes full of wonder, seeming to say, "Look what I found." He was just over six months old at the time, and now, many years and hundreds of grouse later, he is gone.

Ox's first bird, shot a half mile to the north, was much less dramatic. He pointed at a blackberry tangle hard against some red pines. I walked in, out lumbered a bird, and I shot it. When it fell, Ox bolted up to the bird but refused to bring it back to me. Instead, he dead pointed (repointed) it on the trail, so I picked it up and put it in his mouth. Interested more in live than dead birds, he was never much of a retriever, and I never forced the issue as long as he showed me where the downed birds were. Ox's last bird I shot a couple of hundred meters east of his first, the wad from the shell sticking in its side. At the time, just a few days before gun deer season, I had no idea that that would be his last, which is reason to celebrate each and every one.

These acres of tag alders, popple (*Populus tremuloides*, also known as quaking aspen or simply aspen), and red pine are infused with layer upon layer of memory, like onions. I can no longer count the number of birds shot here. One of my friend's setter's ashes lie long scattered in one of the aspen cuttings east of the trout stream, a dog Ox was related to. I shot my first woodcock down by the water, and another friend shot a massive buck here on opening day of gun deer season. Gunnar kicked up a bear here once, and I still taste the tartness of the blueberries growing in that spot I can no longer find. I don't know if it's possible, but my dogs seem to have memories of the place as well.

That morning Ox figured the birds to be down by the water, and so he mucked around in the tag alders along the creek while I walked the ridge above the seep. Off to the north, I could see a high ridge in the county forest blocking out Rib Mountain, and to the west Hardwood Hill loomed in the distance. When my thoughts came back to the task at hand, I heard only silence. Ox had stopped, and then I spied him pointing, framed in the thin popples in his familiar pose. He was hot, his tongue hanging out his mouth and bleeding and his sides heaving. And I knew he had a bird pinned down somewhere in front of his nose.

"Whoa up, Oxie," I said calmly as I worked toward him. "Whoa up." Shouldering my way forward, I forced my way through the crowded trees, most not more than the thickness of a broomstick. Fortunately, he had worked partway up the ridge and wasn't wallowing down in the creek bottom muck. When I got up alongside the dog, I whispered once more, "Whoa up," and just as I passed Ox he pounced and up came the bird. The grouse was on the small side, probably a juvenile and definitely red phased. It hammered across the stream as Ox took two steps in the direction of its flight. Although I knew a bird would flush, the sound and flight set my heart hammering as well. Ox's blood was up, and he circled the spot where the grouse had lain in ever widening circles as though he might have missed another bird.

It was the same act every year, Ox bumping the first bird of the year for as far back as I can remember. He was a stubborn old dog, set in his ways, and so we were equals. When he finally trotted back to me, tail between his legs but fully convinced that he hadn't missed anything, I played my annual part. I grabbed him by the collar, set him back a few yards from where the bird flushed and said, "Whoa up, Ox. That's my bird. Whoa up." Then I moved ahead of him, kicking around in the grass and leaves and hoped he thought I was trying to flush a bird. He stood there, tail down, wagging slowly. He was laughing at me, unrepentant.

After my performance, I tapped him on the head and he raced off, first down into the muck for a muddy drink, then back up the bank. His legs were coated in mire, and deer and wood ticks crawled over every inch of his body. It was time to go home before the sun climbed too high, but we got what we came for—another memory for another day and a taste for the coming season.

Grouse Opener

IN THE NORTHERN HALF OF WISCONSIN, the ruffed grouse season begins the third Saturday in September, often in weather more like July than early autumn. On one particularly warm opener, a friend showed up to hunt with me wearing a T-shirt, shorts, and knee-high rubber boots. I should have taken a picture of his legs afterward, if only to remind him of his lacerated kneecaps. I cooked in my brush pants, but at least my legs weren't bloody. On the other hand, hard frost can occur on opening morning, as it did in 2007 when the temperature dipped into the low twenties overnight.

The grouse opener in Wisconsin is always a bit anticlimactic, unlike the gun deer season's opening weekend when well over half a million hunters infiltrate the Wisconsin woods. Many Wisconsin grouse hunters don't bother with the opener—it's too hot and far too many leaves still cling to the trees, they claim. Better days are coming. A few hunters spend opening weekend at their hunting shacks socializing, a trial run for coming hunts.

Grouse season really cranks up in October, and from its mid-September start the season slowly builds momentum as the trees drops their leaves, starting with the maples and ending in November with the red oaks. By the second week of October, most of the popple leaves now golden, trucks with Ohio, Kentucky, Massachusetts, and a dozen other states' license plates line the streets of Park Falls and Phillips, the traditional state hot spots. October is the peak of the season, and the woods can get crowded.

In September I do get out despite the heat and the green leaves. In 1997, the opening weekend was stifling, the temperatures soaring well into the eighties by midafternoon. Bird numbers were high that year, however, and I had a young dog needing to get into birds, so we went out despite the heat and humidity. It would be miserable in the woods, but I didn't have the wisdom to wait for a better day. The sultry weather didn't seem to concern the dog.

Ox skidded into a point right out of the truck, fifty yards past the gate blocking a logging road that led into the county forest, before I'd even dropped a couple of shells into my shotgun. I fumbled in my pockets for shells while hurrying up alongside the quivering dog. He was young and wild; I had no idea how long he would hold the point. Before I could get up to him, birds started zipping out of the tag alders and the surrounding long grass. They kept pouring out of the brush in ones and twos, more like a covey of quail than a drumming (covey) of grouse.

Sometime during the flurry I fired twice, shooting in the general direction of a multiple flush, making the rookie mistake of flock shooting. Ox, meanwhile, came unhinged and was tearing circles through the cover. I don't know how many birds flushed—a dozen or more. Some crossed the trail into the woods to my right, some bolted directly down the trail, while others flushed unseen into the cover on our left.

Ox was rattled. After the initial bird flushed, he figured it was a free-for-all and dove into the brush, scattering any bird not yet in flight. By the time I'd reloaded, he was still ripping off circles, intoxicated by all the scent and working himself into a July lather. When Ox finally decided to stop circling, he plopped down in a nearby muddy seep and wallowed in the muck like a hog. He was clearly enjoying himself.

After he cooled off, I called him over to me, set him up in front of the tag alders where most of the birds had flushed, and gave him the "WHOA" command. I held my hand palm up a yard in front of him and growled another stern "WHOA." Then I stomped around in the brush like I was flushing another bird. He stood there, bored, his tail low and wagging slightly. After the lesson, I tapped him on the head, the only clean part of his body, and he shot off in pursuit of more scent and more intoxication.

Our day never improved. We saw many more birds, although heard birds would be more accurate, screened as they were by the late summer woods. It felt like we were hunting in the Amazon Basin: lush, green vegetation; stifling humidity; and the incessant whine of insects. For a while I thought we were hunting monkeys instead of grouse.

By noon the sun had reached its zenith in the hazy sky, and by then I'd sliced the arms off my long-sleeved T-shirt, using the knife in my game bag. Sweat dripped off my head, arms, and nose, and our two water bottles had long been empty. I considered refilling them in an algae-scummed pond, but looking at the green water I wondered how dogs can survive drinking such muck. I'd forgotten bug repellant to combat the mosquitoes, which bit Ox mercilessly around his eyes and on his nose, although he didn't seem to mind the blood-thirsty insects. He was hunting—nothing else mattered. My kingdom for a Big Gulp or a Blizzard at Dairy Queen. I prayed for an Alberta Clipper, a cool Canadian high-pressure system, six inches of snow. Ah, come sweet October.

Birdless after a long hour, we turned south toward the truck and were nearly back to the gate, the site of the Herd Flush. In just about the same place, Ox skidded to a stop, head high and tail straight out. Not wasting time, I walked in and flushed the bird, which raced low and away into the tangled alders. I fired once, then again, more at the noise than at a target. The lush vegetation hung so thick on the alders and popples that I couldn't tell if the bird had dropped.

After the flush, Ox roaded in after the bird while I stopped and listened for the telltale flapping of wings, the sound of the last of the life beating out of a ruffed grouse. I heard nothing—yet another miss, I figured. How I dearly wanted to get a bird for Ox, to show him exactly what it was that we were doing out here.

Thirty or so yards ahead, Ox repointed. At his feet lay the bird, a gift from the heavens. I picked the bird up and offered it to Ox, but he just sniffed it while I held the lifeless form. I smoothed out the feathers, marveling at the form and colors of my first bird of the year. That one was enough. I clipped Ox on a lead, and we walked directly back to the truck.

On the drive home, I stopped at a small spring-fed creek that gurgled through a culvert under the gravel road. Ox sloshed down into the cool water, then lay down on his belly on a sandbar and slurped the water. He sported about for a few more minutes before I thought, "Why not?" I looked up and down the lonely country road—no cars—then stripped down to my undies and jumped in, figuring if a car came I would crawl into the dark and cool culvert for cover. But none came, and together we enjoyed the water like a pair of mallards.

The cool, clear water felt almost as good as Ox's first grouse of the season.

The Bird

I N SPRING, AFTER THE SNOW MELTS and before green up, male ruffed grouse stake out their territory and begin to drum in earnest on logs some birds have claimed and used for years. Grouse drum year-round, but it increases in intensity in spring as males seek to attract mates, the drumming reverberating through Wisconsin woodlands, sounding a lot like the thump-thump of an old John Deere two-cylinder tractor. It's a sound I associate with maple syrup, trilliums, and dogtooth violets, the sound of the springtime woods waking after a winter of slumber.

Ornithologists know the ruffed grouse as *Bonasa umbellus*. *Bonasa* means "buffalo." At first thought naming a one-pound woodland bird after a half-ton prairie quadruped seems odd but maybe not if we think of a buffalo's hooves pounding across a dry wash in Kansas, a thundering of hooves similar to the lovesick male's thundering of wings. After all, thunder and drumming are both sonic booms, vacuums created by lightning and feathers. Little Thunderer, we could call our grouse.

Umbellus refers to the bird's umbrella, the conspicuous ruff of feathers at the base of the neck, raised when grouse are mad, aroused, or spooked. Over the years, I've had several females attack me, always during nesting season, with the ruff extended, tail feathers spread out like little turkeys. Once a feisty female pecked me in the foot defending her brood of chicks, and most recently another chased me a good fifty yards before returning to and gathering up her chicks, which I had inadvertently scattered. Another friend, a UPS driver, had a grouse routinely attack her big brown delivery truck at a stop in Shawano County, perhaps because it considered the brown truck competition, although its sense of scale was clearly out of whack. But then so is the sense of scale of a one-pound bird attacking a human.

Grouse also display their ruffs the instant before flushing. Every so often I get a glimpse of a pointed bird on the ground with its ruff up, clucking around slowly, cocking its head back and forth, shifting its eyes, wound up and wired, ready for its instincts to yell *flush*. How can a pointing dog stand so close to the bird, its scent filling the dog's nose, and not pounce? Some can't and break point, trying to grab the bird. Seeing one on the ground, I don't hesitate either. I march in decisively and flush the bird, that lightning flash of a moment, hoping for a sliver of daylight between the trees through which to take a shot. In stands of aspen, spruce, or balsam fir, that's asking a lot.

Wisconsin grouse hunters rarely call ruffed grouse *Bonasa umbellus*. I've heard old-timers in the north woods use *partridge* (pronounced *part ridge*, two words) or occasionally just *pat*, while younger hunters prefer *grouse* or sometimes just *bird*. In Wisconsin, going bird hunting means grouse hunting. *Timber chicken* gets regular use, a derogatory name used by road hunters who view the bird as nothing more than a target, although it does taste like chicken — wild chicken. Hunters also use *timber chicken* in reference to spruce grouse (*Falcipennis canadensis*), which are known to perch in white and black spruce long enough for a person to approach and whack them over the head with a stick. Listed in 1997 by the Wisconsin DNR as a threatened species, these related birds survive in four or five of Wisconsin's northernmost counties.

Some nonhunters have the idea that grouse are basically chickens, close cousins to brainless barnyard fowl. Peter Matthiessen writes in *Wildlife in America* that "gallinaceous birds are no more renowned for their intelligence than are their relatives, the domestic chickens." He thought that the ruffed grouse and wild turkeys had become "relatively wary." Note that he writes "relatively wary," as though they are easy to hunt, like barnyard fowl. Unfortunately for the species, grouse are relatively unwary around motorized vehicles, at times seeming downright stupid. Road hunters have known this for years, and it's a Wisconsin autumn tradition to cruise logging roads, beer in hand, on the lookout for unsuspecting birds along the roadsides, ground swatting them with a shotgun or, for a bit more challenge, plinking them off with a .22. I would think that after nearly a century of this tradition, survival of the fittest would weed out all the foolish birds and their DNA, leaving behind the most elusive of the species to pass on their genes, but some never seem to learn or adapt and are quickly "harvested." I trust they end up on the grills or in the dishes of the shooters because they are a delicacy.

Birds that perch in trees to avoid predators seem almost as dim-witted as those strutting along back roads oblivious to the effects of a shotgun because a bird in a tree is about as easy to pot as one pecking gravel along the shoulder of a county highway. Every season at least one bird pointed by my dog flies up into a tree after I flush it from the ground, thinking itself safe from danger down below on foot. So it perches there, cocking its head, stretching its neck as both the dog and I look up curiously. Every so often Gunnar would bay at a treed grouse as though he were some kind of grouse hound. Once his bark fetched my brother and me a hundred yards to a bird he'd treed. I threw sticks at the bird until it dove out of the tree, and my brother shot it. Gunnar pounced on it when it fell, quite happy to think he had outsmarted that one. Typically, I miss grouse that flush from trees or brush, the uncouth downward flush handcuffing my shooting.

In my experience, however, most Wisconsin ruffed grouse are extremely wary. In all my years of hunting, I've never had a dog seize one on the ground. The fittest birds, in the Darwinian sense, flush well before the dog and I ever get near. I hear many wild flushes, but I imagine more birds sneak away undetected, running away on their strong legs, although with a good dog the chances of this happening lessen considerably. The noted grouse biologist Gordon Gullion felt that a grouse in flight was "in trouble" for the "hazards of flight, including predation and accidental death, usually outweigh the advantages." The old, wise ones know this, which is why they rely on their feet and not their wings. When flushed, grouse seem to have the uncanny ability to put obstacles between their flight and the hunter. Although this undoubtedly happens simply because grouse habitat is so thickly wooded, it seems as though they deliberately do so. The trajectory of a grouse flushing through the woods is inconsistent because while fleeing predators it must dodge trees and brush. Of all upland birds, the ruffed grouse is perhaps the most difficult to hit due to these gunning conditions.

In hand a ruffed grouse loses all the wildness that is so captivating, but it still retains a beauty, reminding me that nature is a good thing. Weighing between a pound and a pound and a half, the ruffed grouse, like just about every game bird except the pheasant, combines hundreds of earthy colors and shades not thought possible when seeing the bird from afar or on the page of a field guide. Colorwise, the iridescent feathers making up the ruff around the neck are the most conspicuous, looking as though they have been dipped in oil. The white and brown breast feathers form a ticked pattern, which contrasts with the darker colors of the head, wings, and back. The long, rounded tail, which can be fanned nearly 180 degrees, like a turkey's tail, contains the most prized feathers. When cleaning birds, I typically save these long, flat feathers used to guide the bird's swerving flight and stash them around the house. Some things are too wild and beautiful to toss away.

Grouse come in a variety of subtle shades, thirty alone in Minnesota according to Gullion. Most hunters categorize grouse plumage as either gray or red, with grays more prominent in the northern portions of their range and reds more prominent in the south, the birds colored in such a way as to match the vegetation of their habitat. When it's flushed, I'm usually close enough to tell if a bird is red or gray. According to my hunting notes over the years, I have shot slightly more gray birds than red, but on many days we return home with both red- and gray-phased birds.

Gullion separates grouse into four distinct color phases—silver-gray, intermediate-gray, brown, and red—using tail feathers to mark these slight variations. Looking closely at the fans decorating my house and cabin, as well as several Ziploc bags of feathers, I see what he means. The reds range from bronze to chestnut to rust; the grays go from silver to smoke and back. In fact, no two birds' feathers are alike, much like our fingerprints or snowflakes. Some juveniles' feathers are barely five inches long, while the longest can range up to seven inches. All are stunning, which is why I have a hard time throwing them away only to decompose in the landfill next to dilapidated TVs, rotting potato skins, and Pop Tart wrappers.

Grouse are found in most if not all of Wisconsin's counties, although they thrive in the northern part of the state, where their numbers are much higher than in the south, where hardwoods rather than popple dominate and the landscape is more urbanized. The northern half of the state, using Highway 10 roughly as an east-west boundary, provides the best habitat for grouse, especially forests managed for popple both private and public.

Grouse prefer wildness, not the typical Wisconsin dairy landscape or unbroken wilderness. Some human intervention, particularly small-scale logging, actually increases their numbers, and wildlife biologists claim the state has more grouse now than it did two hundred years ago when virgin pine dominated the north woods. Aspen regenerated where much of the virgin white pine stood, creating ideal grouse habitat, although, as Wisconsin's paper industry continues to contract and the demand for popple shrinks corre-spondingly, Wisconsin grouse numbers might tumble as well. Nei-ther farm country nor virgin timber offers the cover and food sources grouse need, the birds thriving along the edges of forests we create. The paper and timber industries were and are good for grouse.

Wisconsin's forests are crisscrossed with endless miles of logging roads, two-tracks, and game trails, and I frequent these pathways to get deep into the woods, into secret places I would not go if not hunt-ing, places well off the beaten path even though signs of civilization might be around the corner or within earshot. Grouse, like trout, live in beautifully wild places, proof that our world can be a good place. They take me out of the workaday world into the October and No-vember wildness and draw me back to a place that feels right, making sense of this sometimes senseless place we have fabricated.

Dogless

YEARS AGO A FRIEND FROM Manitowish Waters invited me up to Vilas County to duck hunt on opening weekend. He claimed he was out in the woods one day in early September and happened across a lake loaded with ducks near Michigan's Upper Peninsula. "Thousands of ducks. More ducks than I've ever seen on one lake," he declared. I divided by ten and subtracted one hundred, but even then figured there might be a few ducks left over, so I drove up to hunt with him. Besides, I hadn't seen Chad in some time, and duck hunting tends to be social.

My friend wasn't exaggerating, though; thousands of ducks plied this secluded twenty-acre pothole. I'd never seen so many ducks on so little water and probably never will again. In just a few minutes, we each shot our limit of ducks for the day, and not much later my friend announced that he had to leave to attend a funeral. Our planned day together was over in a matter of minutes, and soon Chad was waving good-bye and backing down the logging road we had driven in on. "Now what?" I asked myself as I walked back to my truck alone. I had left both of my aquaphobic grouse dogs back home.

Since I'd driven nearly two hours north and thousands of acres of public land surrounded me on an early October afternoon, I decided to check out a few logging roads and do a little grouse hunting. Even though I was dogless, I didn't want to pass up prime grouse cover in northern Wisconsin. Scrounging around in my truck, behind the seat, beneath the seat, in the glove box, I found a handful of lead shells and replaced the steel waterfowl loads in my vest. Maybe I'll kick up a bird or two, I thought.

I didn't want to drive back home to concrete and bright lights, where I find it increasingly difficult to remain content. During autumn the house, the backyard under the spreading oaks, the bench down by our beehive—none of these spaces offers the solace or the pull of the October woods. At times I can't force myself to stay out of the woods despite my other duties, its siren song too sweet to resist. When I go there, I feel as though I'm in the right place alongside the flora and fauna. Tramping along the ridges and down in the swamps and seeps, being a predator for once, I look for the wild in me.

Dogs, I anthropomorphize, sense the change better than I do. They hear the call of the wild loud and clear and ache to respond, to become the predator wolf from which they were tamed and finally domesticated. Jack London, in *The Call of the Wild*, writes of "the many-noted call, sounding more luringly and compellingly than ever before"—for hunting dogs, an overwhelming call they willingly obey given a chance. For this reason, I feel sorry for hunting dogs that never get a chance to hunt, that are chained to a stake or pace up and down, back and forth, in a cramped apartment all day until the hunger for the wild dies in their eyes, their owners too domesticated to even notice.

Dogless that October morning, I hiked for over an hour down logging roads and through popples and kicked around in some promising hazelnut bushes. In total, I put up four birds, one from a head-high tag alder so close I could have reached out and touched it with the barrel of my shotgun. While my mind was elsewhere, it bolted down an old two-track and then banked sharply to the right and angled into the woods. A dog would have scented, located, and if things went right, pointed that grouse long before we closed on it, pulled along by a thread of scent. Even off the ground in brush or a tree, my dogs will warn me there's a bird around. They won't always point such a bird, but their body language yells at me to get ready, and usually I am. Dogless and clueless that afternoon, I never got off a shot. I didn't even shoulder my shotgun.

That day it struck me that with a pointing dog I mostly drift through the woods, wandering from place to place, trusting their instincts, their understanding of birds and cover, sometimes with an unloaded gun, often lost in my thoughts, which drift on the wind like falling leaves. While hunting I keep my dogs in focus and in mind, albeit rather obliquely much of the time, their noses substituting for my nose, their noses "seeing" the landscape and the birds therein. They are the text I read when I hunt, the translators of the woods, the link between the bird and me. Half wild and half domestic, they connect domestic man with a wild bird in wild land, listening to the voice of their master and yet pulled toward that more ancient world from which they once rose. It is a curious position my dogs occupy, ravenous carnivores who dine chiefly on Fleet Farm dog food, and even though they have no idea of the limbo they live in, I can see it clearly. Before industrialization and modernization, we were more like them, and it satisfies me to think that for a few hours in the fall I try to find my way back to that older world, "re-creating" what once was, looking for the wild man within. Even so, I fully recognize that my feet are firmly planted in the twenty-first century.

Hunting dogs come alive in the field or the woods, their instincts and spirits awakened in and by the wild, and to deny them this part of their being and such intense and unmitigated pleasure seems unfair. For most of that day, though, I simply missed their presence: the boundless joy, tireless gait, and inbred love of the hunt. Their flowing stride, their rippling thighs, their jingling bells, their happy feet. Most days I hunted just to watch them hunt. On that October day years ago, I learned a valuable lesson: given the choice between dog and shotgun, I'll take the dog every time.

In Praise of Old Dogs

JUST TEN MINUTES INTO THE HUNT, our first of the year, my Weimaraner started to lurch from side to side. Stumbling ahead a few more yards, Gunnar collapsed on his side, legs jerking, eyes wide and staring off into the netherworld for all we knew. We could do nothing but pet him and tell him everything was OK as we waited out the spell wracking his body. This was a big lie because everything was not OK. Gunnar had a bad heart murmur, and when he ran hard he was prone to collapsing. His condition was worsening as he approached thirteen, although none of his spells had been as bad as this one.

We kept him lying down for a few moments until he picked up his head and looked around, puzzled. As he had laid there spasming on the trail, I made up my mind—that was it, no more hunting for him. He had had twelve good seasons, and we had shot a lot of birds over him, mostly grouse and woodcock but also pheasant and quail. Most good things do come to an end. I just didn't expect the end to be looming so close, peering at me through the surrounding screen of trees.

Gunnar got up when he could a few minutes later, and we ambled slowly down the trail back toward our cabin. "That's it, buddy," I said on the way home as he plodded along ahead of me, mercifully oblivious to his condition. "No more hunting for you." The grouse and woodcock season, which had been so promising a few short hours ago, looked at that moment dark and dismal. My other dog, Ox, was eleven years old at the time and still fit, but he, too, was clearly slowing down, with cloudy eyes, growing deafness, and an arthritic left front paw that had left him Rimadyl dependent. Grouse were cycling up, and my dogs were both winding down.

"When are you going to get a puppy?" Friends and family had been pestering us for some time about getting a puppy and replacing the old guard, but after Gunnar's episode we heard this with increasing frequency. The question set me thinking, and I stopped at the home of a breeder a few weeks after Gunnar's collapse to look his dogs over. He had one nine-week-old setter female left. She was cute, came from proven lines, was just what I wanted, but I couldn't put her in my truck and drive her home.

My loyalties lay with my old dogs, and not a new puppy. They'd hunted hard for me for over a decade, and they deserved the chance to get into the field as often as their tired old bodies would allow. We wanted to give them every chance to do so. Besides, they were both a couple of confirmed bachelors, each set in his own ways, wearing ruts in our wood floors as they had worn ruts in our lives. A fresh puppy would have thrown what balance we had in our lives off kilter.

A new puppy would signal the beginning of the end of all our good years together—all those hunts, the birds and the places where we shot them. Behind all that was the salient fact that I had aged right alongside my dogs, clear enough if I looked into a mirror. I wasn't so old that I was counting my age by the number of dogs we'd owned, but my odometer wasn't spinning backward either. Sometimes when I gave the dog his Rimadyl after a hunt, I simultaneously popped a couple of ibuprofen.

A few weeks later, in the early part of October, I rethought my decision. Maybe it was the weather, but if I were Gunnar, I thought one day watching him loaf around the backyard, I would want to hunt even if doing so meant my death. Keeping him home safe and sound curled up on the sofa was selfish on our part. I told a friend I was thinking of hunting him again, and he said, "Make sure you bring along a shovel." My wife thought this comment callous, but it was sound advice. A quick death in the field doing what he loved seemed a more fitting end than one last long, slow trip to the vet. I really needed to consider what to do if he collapsed or died in the field, so I began to carry a length of rope in my game bag and made sure we hunted as near to the road as possible, although at times we did get carried away and went into the woods deeper than we should have. But that's what chasing wild birds does to hunters.

One particularly fine day Gunnar and I had good luck and kept putting up grouse, and each one pulled us deeper into a section of county forest we hadn't hunted in years. The growing distance back to the truck would briefly cross my mind, and then Gunnar would start to work another bird and I'd tag along behind. Neither of us could resist. As we hunted deeper into the woods, my mind started to layer the past years over the present moment. Even though the cover had changed, the popples growing taller and thicker, they couldn't obscure the points and flushes and shots of long gone Octobers and Novembers. Gunnar was a young, lean dog then, full of vinegar, without the scar on his ear and the fatty tumor in his armpit, and I didn't have a chronically sore right shoulder and a bunion on my right foot.

A hard point brought me back to earth, and after a flush and a shot Gunnar fetched up the dead bird. As he moved toward it, a frightened and confused doe arose from the long grass at his feet, and instead of fleeing out into the empty marsh in front of us, she came right back at us, like a fullback bulling through a defensive line on fourth and one. Frightened and confused, she ran right over Gunnar, flattening him. He was stunned and got up yipping and holding up a front paw, a muddy hoofprint on his front left shoulder as clear as a deer track in snow. After realizing he was OK, I couldn't help but laugh. Then I remembered the grouse, and there it was, lying almost at my feet. I'd nearly stepped on it. After picking it up, we started back to the truck.

From then on, Gunnar rode up front with me in the cab instead of in his kennel in the bed of the truck. For one thing, it was easier to hoist him up into the cab than it was to muscle him up on the tailgate. I still had to help him jump up onto the seat, but it was a considerably shorter jump than into the back of my truck. A friend bought a ramp so his old dog could get into his kennel in the bed of his pickup, but after thirteen seasons I figured Gunnar deserved to ride up front. Like a karaoke star, I sang "Gunnar Got Run Over by a Reindeer" as we drove home, and later I took several pictures in the backyard to help us remember the day.

Ox, my English setter, hunted with me the majority of that season, going out three or four times for every time Gunnar did, even though that year Ox was nearing twelve. He had struggled with an arthritic front leg for years, so we iced it after hunts, and he got Rimadyl before he went out and sometimes the next day. We could no longer hunt him all day several days in a row as we had when he was younger and there was no quit in him. He also slowed his pace and no longer attacked the brush like he once did, but that was a blessing because my pace had slowed with age, and following an old dog through tag alders or a young cutting was much easier than keeping up with a young dog in rough country. His mellowing made him a better hunter and definitely more enjoyable to hunt behind.

That season I became more selective with my hunts. If the weather was poor—heavy rain or high winds—I might stay home. If I had a couple of hours after work, I didn't rush home all afire to get in a quick hunt, and we resisted all-day marathons like those we had enjoyed in my dogs' prime years. In their youth, they could hunt all day, get up, and do it all over again the following day. In the early part of the season, before the heat of the day, we would try to get out right after sunrise and we might be done before noon, which meant I might have time to take in the Packers game. Or rake leaves.

My dogs lost their hearing as they aged. I saw this coming, and taught them hand signals—nothing much, just left, right, here, and whoa. Our hunts got a lot quieter, and I'll teach my next dog hand signals much sooner to save my vocal cords. I do have to pay more attention to the whereabouts of my dogs, though, since they can't even hear the whistle most of the time. When the tinkling of their bells grows fainter and fainter, I now go after them, knowing that they could get lost.

In one of his last seasons, I lost Ox in the woods for half an hour or so. After firing my shotgun into the air the second time in the hope that he would hear the blast and come running, my chest started to tighten and my mind raced uncontrollably. *Where is he? He could be anywhere in these thirty thousand acres. Are there wolves around here? What if I can't find him before dark?* Telling myself to think and not panic, I was about to throw down my coat in the hope that Ox would come across the scent and curl up on it when I heard a faint ding—the scratch of the clapper on the side of the bell. "Ox! Ox, here." I tore off in the direction of the sound. Spotting a flash of white, I sprinted through the young popple cutting, as fast as one can run through a maze, toward the white. Ox was pointing a woodcock, maybe fifty yards from where I fired the second time. He'd held it all that time and was still standing there, panting hard and tail hanging low. After flushing the bird and following its flight, I hugged him. He wanted to hunt some more and didn't seem all that thrilled about the hug, but we turned around and headed for the truck. That was enough for that day, another story for the coming years.

We did hold off getting a pup until after Gunnar died. His last autumn he seemed to get older by the day. His hips didn't want to work in the morning when he got up, so I would grab his collar to help him down the stairs. He needed to go outside much more often, sometimes in the middle of the night, but he deserved all the comfort and care we could give. In late October, when he could no longer lift himself off his dog pad and shook from the pain of his cancer, we said good-bye and put him down. I remember the awful beauty of that late October day, a few white clouds drifting in the blue sky and Gunnar's head just visible over the seat, looking as if he were setting off on a hunt.

And so now we start over with a new pup who has reintroduced us to the patter of happy feet on wood floors, shredded shoes and gloves, and seemingly limitless energy. First come the house and yard training, and, since we lost Ox a few weeks after we brought Fergus home, he will be it. No doubt the pup will bump several birds in his first hunting season, and it will be maddening to watch them fly off into the woods without firing. I did check to see how many grouse we had in the freezer since I'm expecting a lean year with a dog that will be seven months old when the season opens. It will be difficult not to compare Fergus with his elders and difficult not to wish for an old, steady dog. Nevertheless, he has pawed his way into our hearts and lives as he writes his own stories.

Scolopax minor

ONE OF MY SHARPEST WOODCOCK MEMORIES is of an unfortunate bird hanging from a power line, its bill trapped in the braided high wire. It looked as though it had been executed or strung high up there by a sadist. It was early April, and the bird had certainly been migrating north along the road, probably at night, when it crashed into the wire and somehow hung itself. What are the odds of a woodcock jamming its bill between the strands of braided wire? Higher than I thought at the time because years later I saw another unfortunate woodcock hung in the same manner.

A few days after seeing my second hung woodcock, Susan brought a Beanie Baby home from the grocery store. She had to have it, she said, it was so cute. With eyes too low and too far forward, wings too stubby, and a smidgen of green in its coloring, its name was Beak, and it's too cute and cuddly to be a woodcock. But the toy maker got the beak right, a worm dipper that unmistakably says "woodcock."

Years later I learned that this long beak is perfect for probing moist soils and grasping a wriggling worm. In fact, *Scolopax minor*, loosely translated, means "the little bird with the beak." Up until about 1990, scientific literature called the American woodcock *Philohela minor*, which again, loosely translated, means "the little bird that loves the swamps."

Its beak is surely its most conspicuous feature, but a woodcock is made up of several other odd pieces. At least one Native American story claims that the woodcock was the last animal the creator made. Using all of the leftover parts, he created what is arguably the oddest bird on the continent. Besides the long beak, its eyes are conspicuously far back on the head, so far back that a woodcock can see predators approaching from most angles. Its ears are where the eyes should be. Its brain is upside down in its head, which might be why wildlife agencies and departments of natural resources consider this migratory bird an upland species, a category reserved for birds that typically stay at home and don't migrate, not like the woodcock, which winters in places like Louisiana and Mississippi.

Ornithologists changed the name to give the American woodcock the same genus as its cousin, the European woodcock, *Scolopax rusticola*: "the beak from the rustic or rural lands." This bird is about half again as large as the American woodcock, and much of our tradition of hunting this bird comes from across the ocean. In France and Quebec, the bird is *becasse de bois*, "the beak of the forests," or simply *becasse*, "the beak." The first Frenchmen who tramped about in Wisconsin in the seventeenth century, the voyageurs, were familiar with the bird, a smaller version than the European one, because they frequently flushed it in their travels through the north woods.

In Italian, the European woodcock is *beccaccia* or *Il Regina del Bosco*, "the queen of the woods," and in German *waldschepfe*, "the forest beak," very similar in translation to *becasse de bois*. To the English, the bird is just the woodcock or cock, from whence the name cocker spaniel derives, the flushing dog that once upon a time worked these birds until it was bred into house dog status. I do have two friends who still use cocker spaniels occasionally on grouse and woodcock, with good success they say. The woodcock has dozens of other names: timberdoodle, mud bat, bog sucker, Labrador twister, night partridge, worm eater, and shit poker or shitepoke. Frank Woolner suggested we change timberdoodle to whistledoodle, although that's hardly an improvement. Woodcock sounds best.

These names refer to the bird's haunts and habits. Woodcock do fly about at dawn and dusk, and to the inexperienced they can look like bats, though the long bill is obvious to the trained eye. Woodcock do love damp places, the alder seeps and marshy fields, where they dine on worms, eating rather voracious amounts at times. Several hunters have told me they refuse to hunt woodcock because of their dietary habits, but on those grounds they shouldn't eat turkeys either, which seem to think manure spreaders are catering trucks.

Woodcock and ruffed grouse are strange bedfellows, but nevertheless they are both species inhabiting much of the same cover. More than once I've flushed a grouse and a woodcock from the same point. At habitat, however, the similarities end. The woodcock migrates up to two thousand miles each spring and fall, while the grouse rarely moves outside its square mile of home ground. The woodcock seems to have steely nerves, sitting tight and relying on its camouflage to avoid predators, while most ruffed grouse would rather do anything than hold for a point. Woodcock rarely flush wild or escape before the dog has a chance to point or the hunter is ready to fire. Mannerly birds, they hold for most points.

Woodcock typically flush in a generally vertical direction, fluttering up into the treetops, while grouse thunder off horizontally in a devil-be-damned manner regardless of what lies in their flight path. A woodcock flush never rattles me like a grouse flush can. Woodcock are small birds that fit neatly into a hunter's palm, while grouse are heavier bodied, traditional upland birds. Woodcock breasts are dark and livery, somewhat like those of ducks or geese, which also migrate; grouse breasts are a delicate white. Both make fine but dissimilar dishes.

Ruffed grouse attract mates through drumming, which, although a peculiar behavior, doesn't compare to the woodcock's eccentric mating flight. Aldo Leopold called this behavior the "sky dance." Most of us have never witnessed this phenomenon, even though we might live just yards away from the dancing grounds. Most Wisconsin woodcock hunters haven't seen it either. We have taken several of our neighbors to a field near our cabin where the woodcock dance every spring, and the sky dance has become our annual entertainment. The male begins the dance in a clearing in a wooded area around dusk, emitting a series of peents, an insectlike sound. It's also similar to the sound a nighthawk makes as it hunts insects in the twilight summer sky. After a dozen or so of these peents, the woodcock lifts off the ground in a twitter of wings and circles up into the sky. Once he reaches an altitude of three hundred feet or so, he warbles liquid notes nearly impossible to imitate or describe. After thirty seconds or so of this warbling, the woodcock drops to the ground like a fluttering maple leaf, returning to the site where he previously peented. He repeats this until it's too dark for us to pick out his body against the dimming horizon, the show over until the next evening.

Other than its bill, the woodcock's most prominent feature is its large brown eyes, set above the bill toward the back of the skull. Four dark russet bands run across the top of the back of the head, the first band connecting the eyes. Fat little birds, a woodcock's camouflage, the complex combination of its feathers and their colors, blends the bird in with the surrounding duff on the forest floor: decaying aspen and alder leaves, withered grasses, sticks, and branches. Its colors subtly combine rust, cinnamon, cream, black, gray, and white and a hundred other shades better painted than photographed.

I try not to look at the eyes, especially when dispatching a wounded bird. Those times, I wish shoot-and-release hunting were a possibility in this world of ours. It's then that all my misgivings about hunting, as well as the barbs of the antihunting rhetoric, creep into my thoughts as the bird shudders and twitches to its end. Like the hunter holding a dead bird in hand in Turgenev's *Sketches from a Hunter's Album*, I say to no one in particular, "Am I not a grand

fellow?" My dogs, on the other hand, sleep with a clear conscience, having no such qualms or second thoughts about death.

Many times I just march in, flush the bird, and follow its twisting flight through and over the popples or tag alders without shooting. Other times I swing my shotgun on the bird, but my finger refuses to pull the trigger. Hunting companions ask, "What are you doing? Your safety snag up?" I shrug and say, "I don't know. I guess I just didn't feel like shooting."

But I do know. I don't like to kill a lot of woodcock even though they are delicious, particularly in the rumaki my wife makes with them. Like Leopold, I love to hunt woodcock but know they are a fragile species, easily overhunted. Their habitat shrinks every year, lost mostly to development, and this destruction is pushing their numbers lower. A November 2008 *National Geographic* article also illustrates how many migrating birds, including woodcock, fly into tall buildings in urban areas during their flights. An incalculable number die this way.

Since I've witnessed the sky dance, a few woodcock every season are enough. Some year, I suspect, I might give up shooting them altogether, content just to watch them twitter off out of sight.

Ox

ERHAPS IT WAS A MATTER of false expectations, of building sand castles in the air, of counting chickens before the eggs had even dropped into the nest. In October of 1996, we bought an English setter pup from a friend and hunter who had been breeding and hunting setters in north-central Wisconsin for years. Although our decision to buy the setter pup was a hasty one, we have never regretted it.

Ox was four months old when we drove out to pick him up, a dark, tricolored setter some people have mistaken for a Gordon setter. The breeder's five-year-old son, Casey, in a sudden fit of inspiration while the family was driving down the road, had named the pup Ox. We decided to keep the name—it seemed to fit the dog and sounded bold and sharp when yelled. At eighty-five pounds, Ox was, well . . . oxlike.

Twice potential buyers had spoken for the pup, even put money down, but for whatever reason hadn't followed through. Maybe it was his unusual coloring or maybe it was happenstance. Serendipity, my wife says.

Ox came from proven lines, Twombley and Old Hemlock, setters from old New England lines. I'd hunted over his uncle and heard tales of other uncles and his grandfather. We knew his parents Boone and Hope. In short, he had the promise of good breeding and a blank slate.

In the spring I started to train Ox in earnest, mostly the basics, the WHOA and HERE commands. He was plenty birdy, with an unquenchable desire to hunt. He'd hunt anything: turkeys, rabbits, chipmunks, june bugs, and butterflies. Later, in early August, we went back to the breeder, who helped me break Ox on pigeons. After a few sessions, he was steady to both wing and shot, solid as we flushed the bird and fired overhead. So we took him down the road a mile or so from the breeder's home to see what he would do on wild birds.

We got him into woodcock along the Rib River, in the tag alders along the river. A few minutes into the cover, Ox locked up, black and white tail straight out and twitching ever so slightly. This was the moment I'd been training him for, and I wasn't disappointed. I stood motionless, the intensity of his point making my eyes well with tears. "Well, there's your bird," Dan said matter-of-factly. "Are you gonna just stand there or walk in and flush it?" Thousands of points and years later, the magic of the point still thrills me, and, although Dan was rather nonchalant about Ox's first point of a wild bird, he seemed equally pleased.

Ox pointed two more woodcock, but later, farther down the river, he bumped a skittish grouse. Then another grouse vaulted from the tags directly overhead, and we jumped, it flushed so close.

In time Ox would learn to handle these wary birds. Regardless of the bump, I was pleased with his performance.

As we were driving away from the river, Dan suggested that I run Ox in an upcoming local field trial. "I'd maybe even run him in the championship round," he said, as we bounced along down the rutted road. I said I'd think about it, but I felt that the puppy stakes would probably be enough for both of us. After all, I had just a little experience training dogs and no experience field trialing. Ox was just as green.

And so we trained even harder. I got Ox into grouse and woodcock about every other day, especially when the weather was cool. By the end of August, he was solid on nearly every bird he encountered—grouse or woodcock. He ran hard and maybe a little too big for my taste. But he held birds. Which led to my decision to enter him in the trial and ultimately my delusions of winning first prize, Ox and me state champions, posing with a tall trophy between us, the envy of all.

The trial was held in early September, the weekend before the season opened. We arrived at the trial grounds and set up next to a truck with Massachusetts plates. *What have I gotten myself into? This is serious business.* I felt like leaving, but I'd already paid the entry fee, so we stuck it out. We were given our time (11 a.m.) and place to run, then settled in to wait. I staked out Ox under some trees and made sure he had plenty of water as the temperature approached 70.

It was close to noon when the judges, both flushed and sweating, met us at the appointed cover. We would be the last pair—Ox's bracemate was a Drahthaar—to run in the puppy stake, and one judge mentioned there had yet to be a point. My heart leapt. Surely

Ox would find a bird. And if he ran across a bird, he would point and hold it. I'd brought along a blank pistol for effect, to show the judges that Ox was also steady to wing and shot. *We have this trial all but wrapped up.*

Ox worked over that cover in the twenty minutes allotted. He slashed right and left, cutting through the cover, head high, tail flowing behind, ears flapping. At one point he cut his tongue on blackberries, and blood streamed down his dangling tongue and onto his black and white chest. The judges called time-out and asked if I wanted to keep going. I squirted water into Ox's mouth and released him, and he bolted off into the cover. Ox didn't know the meaning of *quit.*

He responded to my commands, worked right and left. Surely he would find birds. But then doubts started to creep in as the minutes ticked away. The popples looked a bit overmature—they would have made good firewood—and we were working with the wind instead of into it, which brings the scent to the dog. Then I saw a fresh dog print. *Dogs have already been in here today. How can that be?*

When the twenty minutes ended, we had encountered no birds. Not once did Ox even get birdy. Thoroughly dejected, I started to wonder why I'd signed up for the field trial in the first place. Still I hoped the judges had been impressed with Ox's stamina and drive. He'd worked every bit of the cover, slashing and quartering, running hard despite a bleeding tongue. And since no other puppy had recorded a point, I still felt we had a chance as we walked out of the woods.

Later that afternoon, as my wife and I sat inconspicuously in the rear of the awards ceremony, the winners were announced, and I sensed Ox wouldn't be among them. He wasn't. All the prizes in the puppy stakes went to dogs that bumped birds on the rationale that they had found birds. I got up and stalked back to my truck, kicking dirt clods the entire way and muttering to myself. *In a pointing-dog trial, isn't bumping a bird considered something against and not for a dog? Strike one? Most mutts from the Humane Society could flush birds, too.*

Now, there's a whole lot of subjectivity in field trials—that I understood. I teach English and journalism, and grading essays and articles is a subjective task if ever there was one. But in doing so I try to set and maintain standards. And if pointing a bird at a pointing-dog trial isn't a standard, then what is? Essentially, winning depended on whether the cover allotted held any birds since the puppy stake seemed to be a matter of simply locating them. Too bad if the dog didn't get good cover.

I almost turned around to demand an explanation from the judges and the organizer of the trial, but for once I kept my mouth shut. Inside I was boiling. On the other hand, I was intimidated by the field trial mystique. Who was I to question the judges? Back at the truck beneath the shade, Ox didn't seem to have a care in the world. He was sleeping on his side and merely shifted his eyes to us when we walked up.

We packed up and left. On the drive home, I ranted and raved, cursed our luck and howled into the wind while Susan listened with growing impatience. After a while she said, "You sound just like a Little League dad. Get over it. Besides, the winner only got a teeny-weeny little trophy and a bag of dog food."

Still I kept yammering, complaining about the good hard cash I had wasted (not true—the money would go to improve the field trial grounds), how I could have better spent my dollars on shells or a new pair of brush pants. I kept up the whining for the next week. I could still see the snapshot of Ox and me, a three-foot trophy between us, blue ribbon around his neck.

I took Ox out the next weekend, the opening of grouse season. We went in the cool of the evening since the day had turned unseasonably hot and humid, as mid-September days in north-central Wisconsin sometimes do. In an hour or so, Ox pointed seven woodcock, but their season didn't open until the following weekend. I flushed each of those birds and watched them fly away.

As we turned around to hunt back toward the truck and home, Ox pointed at some blackberry brambles and withered ferns. The brush rustled, but Ox held. *Rabbit?* I walked in, and a small grouse flushed straightaway down the logging road between a red pine plantation and a popple cutting. It even flew east, away from the setting sun. It was the kind of open shot that graces the covers of magazines but rarely happens in the field.

When I pulled the trigger, the bird folded and feathers drifted and floated back down to earth in the shafts of light among the pines. Ox broke, rushed over to the bird, and sniffed it. I urged him the pick it up. After a few sniffs, he did—his first taste of feathers, and they were grouse feathers. With his first bird, the field trial of the previous week quickly faded, along with my false expectations, which, like last April's snowpack, melted away.

Ox had twelve seasons in the grouse woods, and we hoped he would make it to a thirteenth as a role model for Fergus, our new pup. In mid-November of his last season, he came up lame and we took him to the vet. Throughout the winter, he was listless and refused to eat most of the food we offered him. When a dog won't eat venison, it's serious. But it wasn't until March that we discovered he had two tick-borne diseases (Lyme and anaplasmosis) as well as leptospirosis. His kidneys eventually shut down, and we had to say good-bye. He had a relentless drive to hunt, yet he was gentle and kind. He always squealed with delight when we came home. And for that we will always be grateful.

The Cycle

I T'S TALKED ABOUT IN BARS, on sporting clays courses, in operating rooms, even in churches. Magazines publish articles about it, university professors research and write about it, and biologists present their findings at conferences. Every September our local paper runs the same annual article about it, and still we know so little about it—the Cycle, the mystifying fluctuation of the ruffed grouse population that runs its course roughly every decade, crashing headlong from a high to a low sometimes in just one season.

The ruffed grouse population cycle has been called one of the last great mysteries in wildlife management, and biologists have tried to explain this phenomenon with numerous theories, some plausible, others downright flaky. One theory states that parasites weaken birds to the point that other factors—cold and scarcity of food—kill off many of them. This idea comes from English scientists and their work with red grouse, research that may or may not be applicable to America's ruffed grouse populations.

Gordon Gullion, the country's best-known and respected ruffed grouse biologist, has postulated that aspens emit a toxin to protect their buds and keep grouse populations in check. Grouse, finding their favorite buds no longer palatable, seek other foods not as abundant or nutritious. This, in turn, weakens them, making them susceptible to cold, predators, and starvation. This is when goshawks (*Accipiter gentilis*, the gentle hawk), great horned owls, and subzero nights of little or no snow wreak havoc on the population.

In landscapes dominated by aspens, like those of northern Wisconsin and Minnesota, where Gullion did most of his research, the population cycles between high and low extremes. Popple forests are hit hardest and during the ebb of the cycle seem devoid of birds. Covers holding nearly two dozen birds one year could be empty two years later. During some bleak years, I wonder if the birds will ever come back.

Another recent theory links grouse to tent caterpillars, also known as army worms, which denude aspen and oak. Grouse get fat on the two-inch worms, which invade the north woods by the billion. On quiet, windless days, their droppings sound like a soft rain. Motorcyclists have slid out on corners, the road slicked by millions of smashed army worm carcasses. According to biologists, the downside for grouse fattening on army worms is that the denuded trees leave them more vulnerable to their archenemies: the great horned owl and the goshawk. Worms proliferate to plaguelike numbers on aspen, grouse feed on worms (expanding their numbers), and we get the good years. Then hawks and owls move in and fatten on the abundant grouse, whose numbers begin to tumble, and the cycle turns down. In the lean years, grouse hunter numbers follow and tumble accordingly.

Many grouse hunters believe that a predator-prey relationship causes the ebb and flow of the ruffed grouse population. In short, when snowshoe hares become scarce, great horned owls, northern goshawks, and other avian predators exploit the next available food source, which happens to be the ruffed grouse. Some hunters are so sure hawks and owls are gobbling up "their birds" that they shoot avian predators whenever they get the chance. Charles Norris addressed the hawk and owl problem in his *Eastern Upland Shooting*, and his solution was simple: shoot all predators on sight. He wrote, "Only a season or two ago I had the satisfaction of killing one of these hawks (a goshawk), which flushed from a newly fallen grouse. . . . This bird should be destroyed at every opportunity." Leopold, in his early years, also thought that predators depressed game populations. He thought wolves in Arizona were harming the deer population and that no wolves would mean a hunter's paradise, a view he later recanted in his essay "Thinking Like a Mountain." He wrote, "In those days we had never heard of passing up the chance to kill a wolf." Leopold stated that he was young and "full of trigger-itch." After he and half a dozen colleagues pumped lead into a wolf pack, they watched one old wolf die, witnessing the "fierce green fire dying in her eyes." From that day forward, he "sensed that neither the wolf nor the mountain agreed with such a view" toward predators.

Once on a hunt the guy with me wanted to blast a great horned owl out of an oak tree before I talked him out of it. This same guy plugged a porcupine on another hunt, putting five rounds into its body before it dropped from the tree it was debarking and hit the ground with a thud. Nearly as stunned as the porcupine, I kept my mouth shut that time and haven't hunted with him since. Then one of my dogs got quilled, and it happened again a month later. After putting the dog in a headlock, yanking out several dozen quills, and spurting blood all over myself and the decking of the back porch, I at least understood his antiporcupine venom.

Another time a goshawk dove on a grouse we had just flushed, flaring when I fired at the fleeing grouse. I have no desire to go hawk or owl gunning and can't imagine country without these grouse predators, just like I can't imagine the north woods without the wolf. Like Leopold, I think there's a place in our world for nonhuman predators and they have as much right to life as me. In fact, they may have more right to grouse than we do since humans have a much wider range of food sources and choices.

Leopold, in his essay "The Farmer as a Conservationist," suggested that the cycle was the result of poor land management by humans. "Were grouse and rabbits always and everywhere cyclic? I used to think so, but now I doubt it. I suspect the cycles are a disorder of animal populations, in some way spread by awkward land-use." Leopold didn't blame predators, parasites, or toxins; he blamed man, suggesting that somehow we have upset the natural balance so that animal populations never stabilize. They teeter back and forth between increase and decrease because we've monkeyed so much with the landscape and their lives.

Most of the research on grouse claims that hunting pressure has little if any effect on grouse populations and that killing a million birds, as the Minnesota DNR estimated its state did in 2000, doesn't harm the overall population. Biologists call human hunting "ancillary predation." A century ago man killed few grouse and two hundred years ago even fewer. Yet how can our added hunting pressure—our dogs, vehicles, beep collars, and ballistically super shotguns—not have a negligible effect on grouse populations? Some studies found that similar habitat, one section open to hunting and the other closed to hunting, showed little difference in overall population. In fact, the hunted section in such a study in Pennsylvania reported higher populations than the nonhunted section. Game organizations, guides, and the hunting industry in general like to cite these studies, but my common sense tells me to leave a bird or two in the lean years. Each and every dead grouse subtracts something—if nothing else the energy of its presence—from the landscape.

In the end, the Cycle isn't so bad. Besides, there's not much we can do about it. In a way I enjoy the down years since fewer hunters take to the woods, and I don't have to wonder if there will be a car or truck parked in "my spot." According to DNR statistics, about 200,000 Wisconsin grouse hunters take to the woods each year, which means about one in twenty-five Wisconsinites hunts grouse. When the cycle bottoms out and it starts to seem like grouse should be placed on the Endangered Species List, close to 190,000 of these hunters give up and turn to other pursuits: waterfowling, home improvements, repairing deer stands, NASCAR, the Packers. The woods empty out, at least until the gun deer season approaches, and that gives me more room in which to roam about.

The lean years of the Cycle probably benefit woodcock as well since the majority of Wisconsin grouse hunters shoot woodcock incidentally, their seasons and habitat overlapping. If a grouse drought sends hunters to other pursuits, then fewer woodcock will serve as feathered targets, and, unlike grouse, all research points to lack of suitable habitat as the primary reason for the alarming decline in woodcock numbers each year.

When I got serious about grouse hunting and bought my first pointing dog, I was too green to realize that the Cycle had plummeted to its basement bottom. We would go out all day and see six or eight birds, one an hour, and I was pleased; when the Cycle swung upward and peaked, we put up that many birds in forty acres, which made me feel like the wealthiest man in the county.

The bottom of the cycle, that purgatory for grouse hunters, brings forth a hunger for more birds, for better times, which makes the top of the Cycle that much sweeter. Some truth remains in the old cliché that absence makes the heart grow fonder, but then again, who am I kidding? Grouse hunters would like to live forever at the top of the Cycle in an endless autumn of untold birds.

How to Hunt Grouse

IRST, FIND SUITABLE COVER, then start walking. Keep walking. A dog and a good pair of boots help.

In a sense grouse hunting is a simple undertaking, as simple as the previous paragraph. All the state requires is a license, and an older hunter like myself isn't even required to take a hunter safety course, although older hunters could surely learn a thing or two from doing so. For a few dollars each fall, I am licensed by the state of Wisconsin to wander through the woods seeking my prey. But this is a deceptive simplicity.

Outdoor writers have turned out thousands of how-to articles on grouse hunting, enough pages to fill books that would in turn fill a shelf in my library. Reading about hunting, however, can only take one so far, which most of the time isn't much farther than the distance between the garage and the sofa.

Grouse hunting—a practice and a discipline, a religion for a few—requires time, effort, stamina, and years of experience. A hunter must be fit, able to trek comfortably long distances over rough cover.

He or she must know something about this cover, an awareness of which habitat is more likely to hold birds. To be effective, a hunter needs to know how to train and use a dog, forming a partnership that increases the effectiveness of both predators. Skill at handling and shooting a shotgun comes only after years of practice at the trap or skeet course and a good amount of time spent shooting in the woods because a lucky shot is just that, blind luck not to be counted on. A grouse hunter must possess some navigational ability, although GPS, modern wisdom we can purchase, shortcuts the use and understanding of a compass and intuitive pathfinding. No hunting retailers offer these skills for sale.

We can read how-to articles until our eyes blur and our heads ache, but the skills necessary to be a grouse hunter only come with time and practice. At their worst these articles can trick the uninitiated into thinking that the road ahead is smoothly paved with yellow bricks. At its best, however, a how-to article motivates the would-be grouse hunter to lace up a pair of boots and start that long walk through the woods. Shod with my boots, I have yet to finish mine.

MIDSEASON

Flushing Wild

THE BIRD EXPLODED UP FROM BENEATH a screen of balsam firs less than ten yards from the logging road. A jolt rushed through my body like an electrical current, my brain instantly and subconsciously recognizing a ruffed grouse. My body reacted much slower, however. The grouse banged up through mixed popple and balsam fir, clipping branches, evergreen needles, and yellowing leaves, fleeing for its life. Clearing these trees, the bird vaulted into the October blue, set its wings, and planed down the ridge on cupped wings toward the tag alders lining Twenty-six Mile Creek. This was my second wild flush of the day, and I stood there flat-footed, my eyes following its coasting flight down the grade. In the deepening silence, a raven croaked as if in mockery of my turtlelike reflexes.

The dog missed it all, which is why the flush caught me off guard. Ox, my English setter, had worked off into promising cover on my right on the other side of the logging road, and he never saw or winded the bird from over there. Fifty yards away, he didn't even hear the flush. I run pointing dogs because they give me warning—but not this time.

When Ox circled back toward me and across the road, he ran through the lingering scent cone and skidded into a point. He hunkered down, his head lower than his hindquarters, flanks heaving—his usual grouse point. It was beautiful point, the sight of which I never tire, but it was all for naught. After several seconds, he sensed the bird had flown, the scent slowly dissipating, so he slowly relaxed, uncoiling from the intense single-mindedness of his point. "He's gone, Oxie. No bird. He fooled us both." After a few more moments, Ox, convinced the bird had flown, trotted off in search of more intoxicating scent, moving in ever-widening circles away from his point. I continued down the trail as well, moving away from my warm truck and coffee in the thermos, deeper into the woods.

Wild flushes are a part of grouse hunting, of all upland hunting. Before a hunter can even react, the bird is gone, beyond reach and out of range. If the bird flushes in range and an opportunity presents itself, I might snap off a quick shot, but more often than not I don't react and just watch or hear the bird or birds fly off. Every so often time and chance align and I bag a wild flush, but most times I just stand there, caught off guard, my nerves tingling from the sudden jolt. Hunting with a pointing dog and relying on it—that's part of my problem—and if I hunted behind a lab maybe I'd stalk through the woods coiled up like a mousetrap spring, ready to go off at the slightest touch. However, I couldn't maintain such intensity for an entire hunt. Hunting behind a pointer suits me much better.

Like ruffed grouse, most of my ideas flush wild, too. Before I can react, they're gone, racing for cover on some distant ridge or woodland seep. Before I can get them down on paper, they're sailing away across the creek, over the hill, into the next county, glimpses of what could have been . . . if only. If only I had a gun that could shoot down these ideas. If only I had a dog that could retrieve my thoughts and a game bag that would hold them. Every so often I hit one of these ideas and manage to get it home, the "if only" connecting with the "then" of the main clause.

One October day I decided to record my thoughts throughout a day of bird hunting, writing them down as I went so I might relive them someday, perhaps some distant time when I would be too old and feeble to hunt. So I stashed a pen and a notepad in my game bag to record my every thought, stopping every so often to jot down a few words. I thought I'd come up with some sort of grouse-hunting stream of consciousness, my thoughts afield. Plus then I couldn't say *if only* I'd had a pen and some paper out there in the woods . . .

This procedure lasted about fifteen minutes, until the dog winded the first grouse, and I started to act instead of think. We bagged that bird and a few others. The notepad got bloody and full of feathers riding around in my game bag, while the pen fell out somewhere in the woods. And I felt young again. I have always wondered if a crow or blue jay picked up that ballpoint and flew around with its newfound curiosity, or if maybe a raccoon or squirrel gnawed on it until the ink blew up in its mouth. I never did run across a blue raccoon.

As you might have guessed, this was a hopeless experiment doomed to failure. It was a thought that *should* have flushed wild. If only I hadn't thought that one up. But often it's the ill-conceived ideas I capture while the best ones flush wild. That day, though, it did occur to me that I'd much rather hunt than write, or that writing could wait until January's cold and darkness or July's heat and humidity.

Grouse and woodcock hunting is about doing and living, breathing deeply and cruising through the woods, moving along the edges, reacting to game in an ancient way. It's about reading cover and dogs, looking at the world through predatory eyes. I trail after my dogs and their tinkling bells, their noses and legs leading me ever deeper into the woods after things that flush wild. A bird or two along the way also helps, but the thought of just one bird at the end of a point gets me out there—for certainly there are worse ways to squander my time.

While bird hunting, the point is to leave thoughts—those of work, pressing bills, sour relationships, the to-do list, even mortality—back at home. Every time I drop two shells into my shotgun and tell the dog to hunt, I want all my thoughts of the civilized world to flush wild, which isn't always easy for a writer to do, someone whose brain seems to be hardwired to *on*. At the end of the day, whether we like it or not, all those pressing thoughts will come back to us on the drive home or maybe later sitting around the kitchen table—many of which should have long ago flushed wild.

Small Presents

M Y WEIMY LIKED TO HANG OUT in the garage with me while I cleaned birds because he got most of the grouse hearts and livers, which he wolfed down in a single bite. For some reason, he had no interest in woodcock hearts, which are often larger than grouse hearts even though the bird is about a third the size. (This difference stems from the fact that woodcock fly thousands of miles while grouse rarely fly more than a quarter of a mile.) Gunnar would be lost and twitching in a dream on the sofa after a long day of hunting, and yet somehow he could hear me quietly slide open the kitchen drawer to get the game shears. If I didn't get to the birds fast enough for him, he whined and nudged me with his nose until I finally gave in, got up off the couch, and gathered my tools.

Our routine never changed. After spreading newspaper on the garage floor, I pulled the birds one by one out of my game bag and set them nearby. Clip off the wings and the heads, then peel off the breast feathers, which slip off the birds as if I were pulling a T-shirt off over my head. When I opened up the warm and bloody body cavity, Gunnar nosed in, impatient for me to hand out the darkly muscled vitals. He also inspected the crops, which I always opened. Both of us were keenly interested in these bags of goodies (he to see what there was to eat and me to see what the grouse had been dining on) with their slightly fermented buds, seeds, leaves, fruits, catkins, insects—warm, delectable presents wrapped in a skin membrane. When we went back inside, Gunnar invariably had a feather or two stuck to his nose, and we would find these feathers scattered around the house, sometimes months later.

Once I shot a bird with an acorn jammed in its beak. It held on to that nut with a viselike grip, even in death, like a pig with an apple stuffed in its mouth at a medieval banquet. When the dog handed over that bird in the field, I could feel its crop full of acorns, like marbles in a feather sack. Susan didn't believe my story until I showed her the grouse, and when I cleaned the bird later that evening, the acorn was still lodged in its beak. Sixteen smallish acorns filled that crop plus the one in its beak. Seventeen acorns is still a record for me. Greed killed that bird. Weighed down with its burden of acorns, it couldn't flush like a more moderate eater, and the split seconds lost to its heavy load cost it its life. Grouse can't take their treasure with them—not even in acorns.

Gunnar tried to crunch down a couple of those acorns, but he gave up after what sounded like a cracked tooth and waited for me to open up the next crop. He preferred greens over acorns: clover, aspen, or wild strawberry and blackberry leaves. I carried one of those seventeen acorns around in my vest pocket for the rest of the season as a good luck charm. I can't remember if it brought us any luck, but one day that acorn fell out of my pocket, hopefully to be planted by a squirrel in fertile soil.

Another time a similar incident happened—a grouse tried to swallow a crabapple the size of a golf ball. This one's crop was empty, blocked by the large crabapple, and this bird, like the acorn bird, held on to its treasure with a rigor mortis vise, the crabapple still wedged in its beak when I pulled the bird out of my game bag to clean it.

Through the years, I have scanned several magazine articles advocating the examination of crops in the field in order to find the grouse's food source. If grouse happen to be eating hazelnuts, the wise hunter heads for the hazelnut patches, and bingo—the birds will be dining there on hazelnuts. Decades ago an outdoor writer published this idea in a hunting magazine, and now it's an outdoor cliché, parroted yearly in magazines and newspapers and now on Web sites. Find the food source, the theory claims, and from then on a competent gunner can stack up birds like cordwood.

But it's not that simple. The theory would work if all grouse ate all the same foods at the same time, but they don't. Just like people, ruffed grouse eat a wide range of foods, although they prefer some tidbits more than others. During winter and early spring, their diet is more restricted, particularly in the north woods where deep snow covers much of their food. Then popple buds dominate their diets. After the snow flies, I would bet my favorite shotgun that a grouse's crop will hold popple buds. This is not to suggest that in winter they feed exclusively on their favorite bud because they're opportunists and will eat whatever: catkins, winterberries, mountain ash berries, corn from deer hunters' bait piles. Obviously, though, in winter they don't have the variety of the bountiful times of the year, late summer for instance. So I bet on popple buds, playing the odds, and hunt there.

In plentiful times grouse eat a smorgasbord of foods from grasshoppers to blueberries. A grouse's taste is catholic, the bird eating almost any vegetation in the woods that is even somewhat edible. They own curious and adventurous palates. Flying billy goats in gastronomic terms, grouse will eat over a thousand different foods, including poison ivy berries and poison sumac leaves. They eat so many different things that sometimes I can't identify the contents of a bird's crop. Voracious feeders, grouse rarely die of starvation. Once I found a small frog in a crop, and fortunately I didn't open that one in the field and decide to spend the rest of the day searching for frogs, although on occasion when he was bored Ox would point frogs or toads.

That is why checking grouse crops in the field doesn't seem to me like a reliable way to find birds. It's interesting, and surely can't hurt, but more often than not the next grouse a hunter shoots will have something else in its crop. One might be chock full of white dogwood berries while the next could be empty. Or, more often than not, a crop contains several different foods. Then where, according to the old theory, does a hunter turn? Knowledge of cover, even an intuitive one, a good dog, or just blind luck finds hunters more birds.

This is why I prefer to open crops back home, in the company of my dogs, hoarding them like Christmas or birthday presents. We never know what we might find. If I found a dime or a quarter inside, that wouldn't surprise me. If I do someday, I'll string it around my neck and carry it in the grouse woods until I can walk there no longer.

Hunting with Diana,
Grousing Around with Susan

W E HAD A POINT, and it was Susan's turn to flush. She walked in, shotgun at the ready, the butt just below her armpit. When she got a few feet past Ox, a woodcock twittered up batlike in front of the dog. Clearing the dense popples, it flattened out and flew west directly into the sun. Still, she held fire.

When it was a speck on the horizon, her shotgun boomed, and I wheeled around and cried, "NO, NO, NO, NO! What are you doing?" Why did she wait until the bird was nearly out of sight to fire? As I was thinking this, a woodcock tumbled down from overhead through the popples, tinking off branches and nearly hitting the dog on the head. Moving a few feet, he reached down, picked up the lifeless bird and trotted over to me with it.

Susan stalked over to me, a gleam in her eye, and took the bird from the dog. She cradled it in her palm and smoothed out the rust-colored breast feathers. "It's all over now," she said stroking the dead woodcock's head. After a few moments, she pocketed the bird and said, "They're such beautiful birds." Dropping another shell in her side-by-side, she said, "I know what I'm doing. You don't always have to tell me what to do."

Her look was like the one that I imagine Diana gave Acteon when the huntsman wandered into the goddess's hidden sylvan palace. As punishment for his human folly, Diana turned Acteon into a stag. Acteon, realizing he had grown horns and hooves, fled home, and near his gate his own dogs attacked and pulled him to pieces, all while his hunting companions watched and wondered where he could be. Acteon is missing all the fun, they told each other; too bad he isn't here to see this, what a show. I stood there, wordless, looking at my feet and to make sure I wasn't growing hooves. Calling to Ox, Susan moved forward, resuming our hunt.

Susan grew up in southwestern Iowa in a family that raised vizslas and hunted quail and pheasant every weekend of the season. We have a few old pictures, faded color Kodak prints of hunters posing with the take of the day, and often little Susie is there off to the side smiling, although she never carried a gun when she went along. Few midwestern girls hunted in the late 1960s and early 1970s mainly because it just wasn't done back then. After we married, it just seemed natural that she should tag along, and it wasn't long before she wanted to carry her own shotgun.

After reading the essays of Frances Hamerstrom, Aldo Leopold's first female doctoral student, Susan learned that Hamerstrom shot a Parker 20-gauge, a side-by-side. An avid hunter like her mentor

Leopold, Hamerstrom was most likely the first female with a PhD in wildlife biology in this country. A bit later Susan found and bought a Spanish double, a Ugartechea 12-gauge, which fit her exactly, weighed less than seven pounds, and looked remarkably similar to Hamerstrom's Parker boxlock.

Even though attitudes have changed significantly in the last century, women are still a minority in the field, particularly in the uplands. Their numbers in the field are increasing, however, even as the number of male and young hunters declines. When I'm hunting with Susan and we run across other male hunters in the field, many act surprised. Some don't know how to act and virtually ignore her. Once while we were walking a back road, a hunter drove by in a truck, stopped fifty yards down the road, then backed up. He rolled down his window and asked, "Is that a Pempek setter?" Dan Pempek breeds English setters near Athens, Wisconsin, and this guy could tell a Pempek dog on the fly. He got out and talked dogs for some time, all the while petting Ox, the Pempek setter. He never once directed the conversation toward Susan; he wouldn't even make eye contact with her. It was as if she wasn't even standing there on the road with us. After he pulled away, she huffed, "What am I, invisible?" I joked and told her he was intimidated by the blood on your gloves. She looked at them—they were spotted with bright, fresh blood.

In Wisconsin more women hunt deer than any other game, not surprising since deer hunting is by far the most popular form of hunting in the state, yet even so women only made up 8.5 percent of deer hunters in 2009, according to the Wisconsin DNR. Mark Duda

of Responsive Management, a Virginia firm that tracks and inter-
prets outdoors trends, claimed that women bought about 15 percent
of the twelve million hunting licenses sold in America in 2006. The
statistics don't say how often a licensed hunter went hunting, or if
he or she did at all, and my hunch is the typical man hunts more
often (more hours and days) than the typical woman hunter, further
increasing the disproportion.

For one thing, some men simply don't want their women hunting and don't provide them the opportunity to do so. Part of this fear
stems from a male ego afraid of being shown up by a woman in what
is supposedly a man's world. A few male hunters want to keep a lock
on heroism and virility, two characteristics hunters hold in high es-
teem, and an autonomous female in what they consider their world
threatens their masculinity. An independent woman, especially one
with a gun, doesn't fit a narrow and conservative view of femininity.
High heels and makeup, yes, but a shotgun or a rifle, no. The shotgun is a great equalizer, and Annie Oakley with her 16-gauge would
make all of us, both men and women, look silly. Oakley once held
the twenty-four-hour record for breaking the most clay pigeons,
shooting two identical 16-gauge side-by-sides.

Another excuse to keep women at home cites tradition, sticking
to the conventional gender roles that let the girls cook or clean
the game but not hunt and shoot it. The men are hunters, while the
women have always been the gatherers, ignoring biology since the
alpha female hunts in the wolf pack alongside the alpha male.
(Woodcock females, by the way, are generally larger than the males,
which is one way to distinguish their sex. In the insect world, the

female occasionally devours the male, the natural world providing examples of aggressive and wild hunting females.)

The impulse in some males to keep girls out of the club runs deep and has an extensive mythology to back it up, but the goddess Diana stands conservative gender identity on its head, exposing the traditional separation of the sexes when it comes to hunting. Diana embodies both destructive and violent behavior (negative) and nurturing behavior (positive), for she not only carried a bow and arrows but was also the goddess of childbirth and protector of nonhuman nature, that is, the natural world. Many male hunters have difficulty understanding, then accepting, this dualistic nature, which combines the genders.

When Susan and I hunt, our genders occasionally clash. I try not to bull ahead when we hunt together, but often I do, especially when the dog is hot on the scent of a running bird. "You coming?" I yell behind to Susan, who is still fighting her way through the brush. She doesn't like what she calls my moronathons, my all-day forced marches with little food or water. "What's wrong? Just a little farther. I have a Power Bar and some water. It's not that far. Look, the dog wants to go." At times, I get so caught up in the pursuit of birds that I keep going deeper into the woods into places unknown, following the well-known script of man leading a woman off on a wild grouse chase.

The dominionistic model of hunting, a term coined by the writer Stephen Kellert, helps explain much of the male machismo. According to this model, the hunter seeks to gain dominion over nature. To put it bluntly, the hunter goes out to kick some ass, in this case the ass being deer, turkeys, bears, coyotes, ducks, grouse, or whatever happens to be in season. The larger and more ferocious the animal, the greater degree of self-worth or machismo a hunter earns by dominating it (a heavily antlered buck or a large black bear top the list in Wisconsin). This model, which both men *and women* may fall into, also partially explains the wolf hatred running through the state. Since the wolf competes with man for some of the same animals, it needs to be dominated, taken care of for good, according to some hunters. With smaller animals like grouse or walleyes, the dominionistic model manifests itself in numbers. Putting as many birds or fish in the freezer is how a hunter dominates nature, and I find myself falling into this trap occasionally when I consider a successful hunt a heavy game bag. Tallying up kills, birds in my case, demonstrates dominion over the birds of the air. It's a consumptive attitude that sees nature as just another arena we try to control and from which we intend to extract as much fun, protein, and ego massaging as possible.

Susan never speaks of grouse and woodcock in terms of domination, and even for me it's difficult, as well as humorous, to think of dominating a bird that weighs a bit over one pound. She hunts because doing so removes her from an artificial environment and takes her places she wouldn't normally go. We would never muck around in tag alder runs and force our way through blackberry thickets except in pursuit of grouse and woodcock. She once told me that hunting "feels like I'm playing hooky, like I'm walking away from my to-do list."

Another time, while we were taking a break from hunting, sitting on a rock overlooking a creek and eating sandwiches, she said after a few moments of silence, "Sweet grapes." I had no idea what she was talking about. "You know, sweet grapes instead of sour grapes." No, I didn't know. The term came from a book about being childless she was then reading. Instead of mourning our childlessness (sour grapes), the book turned the cliché on its head and discussed all the benefits of being childfree (sweet grapes). It sought to put a positive spin on what is often thought of negatively in our culture. It was sweet grapes for me, too, sitting there with her that day.

Women hunt for other reasons as well. Susan's older sister Cindy, a pheasant and deer hunter from Iowa, talks about the community of hunters and the social aspects of hunting. She delights in the family hunts centered on the Thanksgiving and Christmas holidays. But she mentions more subtle reasons as well. "This may sound weird," she has said, "but when I'm out there I feel like it's who I am. I feel more connected to myself." Like Susan, she feels a deep connection to the earth and has a healthy sense of place, which includes knowing where our food comes from. Both, not coincidentally, are excellent wild game cooks and eat with gusto the dishes they create.

Although I've taught Susan a few things about hunting—things about gunning, bird behavior, and habitat, as well as dog training—she has taught me much more, and those lessons have been abiding concerns. For one thing, I've learned that our perceptions and expectations about hunting vary widely. Usually I favor the frontal attack when grouse hunting, crashing through the brush to get to the dog and the bird, often jogging along when I know the bird is running from points. Sometimes I try to get around the dog and head off the bird, which means I plow through blackberries, popples, tag alders, whatever happens to lie in my path, parting the brush with my shotgun. Susan takes a quieter, more oblique route.

Unfortunately, dogs can scoot through brush much quicker than humans. Their four legs help, but they also don't have as much brush to contend with down close to the ground. In other words, it's a race to keep up with the dog when it's working a running bird. At times I've been so intent on keeping up with the dog that I look up and ask myself, "Where's Susan?" Then I start hollering something like "Get over here. Quick. It's not going to hold all day." The bird comes up, and I shoot, just as Susan plunges through the thicket behind me.

She never seems to hurry. Her idea of a hunt is a saunter through the woods, taking in whatever happens to be at hand: asters in a clearing, an abandoned chickadee's nest, a deer shed. "Did you see those spiderwebs? Weren't they wonderful?" Dumbfounded, I say, "What spiderwebs?" The ones in my head, maybe. "That wolf scat had deer hair in it, didn't it?" Wolf scat? I'm trying to recall the scat, to force the image up out of my subconscious. No wolf scat there, it seems. "It was on the other side of the creek we just crossed. You missed it, didn't you?" I nod.

She has made me see down through the years that there's more to hunting than a limit of birds and a heavy game bag. Although she dearly loves to cook and eat grouse and woodcock, Susan hunts for more than just the kill. For more than just feathers, meat, and blood.

Like Trees, Walking

IN SAINT MARK'S GOSPEL, the people lead a blind man from Bethsaida to Christ to be healed. Christ lays his hands on him a first time and then asks him what he sees. The man says, "I see men like trees, walking." When Christ puts his hands on him a second time, his sight is fully restored. Even though a comma stands between trees and walking in the King James edition and the walking refers to men and not trees, when I read this verse as a kid in Sunday school I imagined trees walking. J. R. R. Tolkein's ents fascinated me, as did the Awakened Trees, which rose up and made war against the Telemarines in C. S. Lewis's *Prince Caspian*. Something as massive and rooted to the earth as a tree actually moving fired my childhood imagination while adding an unsettling quality to the night woods in the backyard and down the block.

The reality of global warming and climate change, however, has tainted the innocence of my childhood dreams. Trees lurch around in our fantasies and literature, but over time and in these days of climate change, they literally travel, some species shifting north in an imperceptible but inevitable march as the planet heats up and the climate changes. When I am driving north from Madison to Wausau, or vice versa, I note the natural shift in the landscape—from the prairie savannas in southern Wisconsin to the north woods, and sometimes I picture the southern landscape moving north and my car sitting still, the landscape rolling by on a conveyor belt. We think of trees as permanently rooted, and as individual species they are. The red oaks in my front yard are over 150 years old, and a white pine outside the bedroom window where I write is at least half that old. These trees have been standing here, rooted to the same spot, much longer than most people have been alive. The oaks are nearly as old as our country. As a species, however, trees are mobile.

Between Stevens Point and Wausau the shift from prairie savanna to the north woods is complete. It's here that aspen and white pine (*Pinus strobus*), begin to thrive, replacing the massive oaks that dominate southern Wisconsin. My imagination pictures these oaks striding north to war against the smaller, more fragile popples (the vernacular for aspen), eventually taking over their territory as they quest north for more land.

Ruffed grouse will migrate north as well, following the popple, the flower buds of the aspen their most important food source. Grouse also use the dense cover popple provides to shelter them from avian predators in particular. To them popple is home and life. In fact, in New England some hunters refer to grouse as popple partridge. Years ago hunters figured out that popple was the grouse's tree of choice in Wisconsin, and as early as the 1930s scientific studies were listing aspen as the most important food source for the bird. A 1952 Wisconsin study reported that aspen buds "were consumed out of proportion to their availability in the forest." In other words, grouse would eat more aspen buds if they were available.

The grouse's penchant for aspen can't be overestimated. If a hunter wants to find grouse, he or she should start with the closest stand of thriving aspen. In winter grouse routinely roost in popple trees for an evening meal, their silhouettes readily identifiable, especially on clear days in the waning and slanting winter light. Often more than one bird will be perching in the trees, plucking off the delicate buds. Grouse hunters know the bird's relationship to the tree and hunt these stands more than any other type of cover.

Popple stands grow, mature quickly, and then either die off, replaced by climax forest, or loggers come in and cut the trees for pulp. Stands I hunted years ago have matured and today don't hold as many birds as they once did. Some hold few if any birds now, while other stands I've traditionally hunted have been logged and are growing back, and these I check yearly as they age to perfection. And every year I discover new stands and new cuttings, marking them on a map for future reference. As a grouse hunter from northern Wisconsin, I have always considered popple more or less part of the landscape, taking them for granted, but global warming has changed my perspective. Our flora and fauna are much more fragile, even though an individual tree seems about as permanent as the stones in the soil around them.

Ironically, my hunting contributes to the warming as I drive to my favorite coverts, burning fossil fuels to get me and the dogs there.

Even though I drive a Subaru and occasionally a small pickup and try to limit my impact on the planet, both still contribute carbon emissions that fuel the warming. It's impossible for me to walk or bicycle to my coverts since most lie beyond the range of my legs or a bike. Slowly, ever so slowly, some hunters have begun to realize that our consumptive lifestyles might actually destroy the very thing we love, and yet sporting magazines are still full of advertisements for gas-guzzling trucks and ATVs. We really haven't made the connection, myself included, between lifestyle and climate change. If only the trees would get up and walk, like Birnamwood when it removed to Dunsinane in *Macbeth*, then finally we might have the eyes to see.

Costumes

I WAS HEADING WEST on the snowmobile trail toward our cabin; she was riding a mountain bike east toward me. We met where the snowmobile trail intersected the middle of the ski trail the woman was riding. Somewhere in the cover behind me, the dog was still hopeful about finding a bird.

"What are you doing?" the woman asked me, staring first at my shotgun, then back at me. She wore Lycra shorts, a cycling jersey, and biking shoes and had a Camelbak hydration pack strapped to her back, the costume of a mountain biker. She rode a carbon fiber, dual-suspended mountain bike with twenty-seven speeds. She wasn't anyone I knew from the area. If I had to guess, I would say that she was from down south, possibly the Twin Cities, maybe Milwaukee or Chicago. The area we were hunting is a popular mountain biking and cross-country skiing destination, yearly drawing thousands of silent sports enthusiasts.

I was about to state the obvious when the dog jumped out on the trail and trotted up to us. When he saw or smelled the woman, he bolted up to her, woofing. She nudged him away with her knee, but he wouldn't be denied and continued to pester her. She nudged him again, but her repulse didn't deter him at all. He thought she was playing with him. I grabbed him by the collar, yanked him away from her and started down the trail. The dog had no business in her face, and she didn't seem like the kind of person who liked dogs. It seemed best to avoid a confrontation and leave. "Are you sure you can hunt here?" she yelled at my back. That was the last thing I heard her say.

A friend of mine always referred to his cycling kit as his costume. He had a closet full of European pro team jerseys and shorts. He even had matching gloves and socks for some of his outfits. At first when he said this, *costume* seemed an odd word choice, but then Chris was forever joking. He never took anyone seriously, not even himself or the sports in which he indulged. But now I'm not so sure the joke wasn't on most of the rest of us since we can take our costumes very seriously. That morning I had on my hunting costume, including the blood on my hunting vest. Ironically, the day before I had worn a bicycling costume and had ridden over the same ground as the woman who was so incensed over my hunting. Had I met her on my bicycle all decked out in a cycling costume, our exchange would have no doubt been pleasant, but as it was she could not get past both my outfit and what I was doing. To be fair, I, too, had on my hunting hat and my hunting attitude, my costume changing my perspective.

A few times each season, I cross the costume boundary and use a mountain bike to save time in hunting isolated covers that require long walks both there and back. I ride with a temporary sling on my shotgun, while the dog runs alongside, and he loves it, loping down the trail no longer hampered by my slow two-legged pace. We might look odd cruising down the trail, me in heavy hunting boots, the dog clanking along with his bell, but we can cover ground quickly and efficiently. For sure this sort of cross-dressing confuses both mountain bikers and hunters. Since we don't fit neatly into either category, people we meet in the woods usually don't know how to classify us, and that often inhibits any sort of dialogue between us since we have a difficult time getting past superficial matters like clothing.

Once while mountain bike hunting in a section of county forest where both pursuits are allowed, I rolled up on a young couple out mountain biking. The dog was thirty yards ahead, leading me down the trail. When I rounded a corner, the couple was petting him, and he was working the free massage for all it was worth. "Is this a Weimerheimer?" the man asked. I said he was a Weimaraner. When he spotted my gun and the tail feathers poking out the front of my vest, his face went cold. Clearly both were uncomfortable with me, although maybe they just didn't like or understand guns. "Can you hunt here?" the woman asked tentatively. I answered yes, this was a county forest and not a park.

"Aren't you afraid you'll shoot yourself," the man asked. Pivoting my shotgun around my shoulder, I showed them that the bolt was open, the chamber empty. "It's unloaded," I answered. Did they think I rode around with a loaded shotgun, blasting away at whatever moved like some sort of mountain bike Rambo? They pedaled away quickly, looking over their shoulders and whispering to each other. They didn't seem sure about me, but they did seem to like the dog, which is a start.

Another time while mountain bike hunting, I ran into a bowman out deer hunting. He told me, "Get the hell out of here." He even nocked an arrow on his bowstring, for my benefit apparently. It seemed he felt as though he owned the public land we were both hunting. I was in "his spot." I didn't argue but thought he was a bit foolish considering I had the shotgun and the dog. Not knowing what to say, I shook my head and rode away, another confrontation not worth pursuing. Had I been driving an ATV, the vehicle of choice for many hunters, rather than pedaling a bike, would he have accosted me? Did pedaling a bicycle and not driving a machine and burning fossil fuels lower me in his estimation?

Actually, it was another bow hunter who gave me the idea of mountain bike hunting years ago. The dog and I were humping it out of a cover, and it was getting dark, but the sky still cast enough light that the trail wasn't completely obscured. We were almost to the parking lot when a light quickly overtook us from behind. The dog woofed a few times, and I clipped him to a lead. Coming up on us with a powerful headlight was a mountain biker who said hello as he passed. His bike was painted camo, and the rider had a bow strapped to the rear rack. The next time I hunted that cover, I rode in and saved myself at least an hour of walking.

Even today when I go on a mountain bike hunt, I feel odd, perhaps because I have a blaze orange hat on my head instead of the protection of a helmet. Susan says it's because I can't multitask. The mingling of two seemingly different pursuits, wearing a hunting costume while riding a bicycle, doesn't sit right with me, even though both give me immense pleasure. It doesn't even register on the minds of my dogs, though. But then they don't put on airs, and they never put on costumes. Every moment of every day, they are simply themselves, dressed and ready to go.

Paul's

ONE OCTOBER EVENING PAUL CALLED, asking about a grouse dish he had once eaten at our home. "You get a bird?" I asked, knowing Paul doesn't hunt. He told me a bird had flown into his picture window, breaking its neck, an untimely death that happens all too often with some species of birds. Grouse, heedless of obstacles when flying through the woods, occasionally crash into windows, not understanding the see-through property of glass.

Paul's house sits on a ridge overlooking the Rib River, and the view out the window gives way to some of the finest grouse cover in north-central Wisconsin. Not a hunter who manages his fifty-five acres for wildlife, Paul didn't groom his woods with grouse in mind. The high grouse population is incidental, the effect of the type of land he owns and the changes he's made to it. He has never heard of Gordon Gullion or his pamphlet *Managing Woodlots for Fuel and Wildlife*. However, Paul *is* a firewood man and a carpenter, and every now and then he cuts a few sawlogs for cash. He's the type of person who needs to be doing something constantly with his hands, building and creating. At last count, he had fifteen cords stacked and drying on his land, enough for about three years' worth of heating in his house and outbuildings. Regardless of what happens, he won't be cold. His firewood cutting and occasional select cutting for sawlogs has helped to create ideal grouse habitat by keeping the woods thinned since he tends to cut the older, more mature trees and leave the younger ones. Older woods where climax species thrive, such as white pines, ancient maples, and oaks, are beautiful and uplifting places, but they are home to few, if any, grouse or any other species that live in immature woods and forest clearings. Deer, bears, wolves, and dozens of songbirds prosper in man-made cuttings that simulate blowdowns and burns, which were common before we started to transform the woods forever with the ax and the chainsaw.

At least a third of Paul's fifty-five acres lies in the floodplain down along the river. Thorn apples, also called hawthorn, tag alders, blackberries, and hazelnuts thrive in this brushy cover, all excellent foods for grouse. The dense brush also protects the birds from predators. Paul loves to cross-country ski and maintains seven kilometers of trail winding through his land and onto his brother's land to the south. These trails meander up and down the uplands to the east then down to the flats along the river, and he has planted them with grass and clover, greens on which grouse can dine. Besides food, the trail creates openings and edge cover for the birds, and the trails also make it possible to ramble around in comfort on Paul's land. Without the trails, a hunter would have to fight foot by cruel foot through the thorns and briars, limiting mobility.

My all-time flush record there is forty-one, an astounding number since Paul's land can be covered in less than two hours. Many of the birds tend to fly across the river to safer ground, and often the cover is so thick I never see the birds to get off a shot, even with a point. Paul's birds also tend to flush en masse because they're so thick, and that raises the number of flushes. In the end, those forty-one flushes might offer five shots. Still, forty-one flushes on fifty-five acres is difficult to believe, nearly one bird per acre, but the high numbers illustrate how grouse can prosper given the right habitat.

For the first few years I knew Paul, I didn't hunt his land. It doesn't have much popple, and so it doesn't have the look of classic grouse cover. It really doesn't look all that birdy, so it never popped into my mind. To get there you have to drive down a half-mile lane through farm fields, all the while dropping toward the river. At Paul's property line, the woods begin, consisting mostly of maple, some ash, red oak, and yellow birch, a wall of trees confronting the surrounding cornfields. Driving this long lane, a grouse hunter would never think that wonderful grouse cover lay just off the road. I had no idea his cover was so ideal, really a grouse paradise, until I was out skiing with Paul one day. A skift of snow had fallen overnight on the ski trails, and Paul had yet to groom them and erase the tracks in the new snow. Just about wherever I skied, grouse tracks crisscrossed the trail—and this was when grouse were in the bottom of their cycle. I was astounded. If there was one bird for every ten sets of tracks on the snow, Paul's land was home to an inordinate number of birds.

"You ever see any grouse out here?" I asked when we stopped for a breather.

"Sure, all the time."

"Like how many?"

"They pop up here and there. I ran one over with the mower last summer."

"You mind if I hunt here sometime?"

"Not if you share the birds."

Down through the years, we have shared many things: tools, wagons, recipes—and birds. Last year I traded an oak sawlog from a tree that fell in our backyard for smaller firewood. Paul happened by when I was cutting up the tree. I was just about to cut into the last twelve feet of the stump, when Paul reached over and shut off my chainsaw. "You're not cutting that up for firewood." It wasn't a question. The red oak trunk was limbless and straight, thicker than the sixteen-inch bar on my saw. Paul took the log home, sawed it up for lumber, and brought me back a load of firewood cut from his land. We've shared work as well, but birds are best to share.

Even in lean years of few grouse, Paul's land always flourishes with birds. When I hunt there, Paul often tags along gunless, usually with a beer in hand. He enjoys these strolls through his woods. Although I've shot dozens of birds there down through the years, I have not diminished the overall population whatsoever. Some studies show that human hunting pressure doesn't affect grouse populations and that our predation is "ancillary," with avian and four-footed predators killing far more grouse than human hunters. Even so, I shoot only a few birds here every season, enough for a meal or two. Good cover affects the population more than hunting pressure, ensuring that grouse will be well fed and protected, even through a long and difficult winter. Wildlife managers and conservation groups, such as the Ruffed Grouse Society, Pheasants Forever, and Ducks Unlimited, know the importance of good habitat, which is why these groups spend millions to acquire, develop, and protect thousands of acres that support their preferred species, although many nongame species benefit as well. Paul cares little about managing his land for wildlife, his habitat more incidental than systematically planned, although he and his family enjoy seeing the turkeys, deer, bears, and songbirds living there.

From Paul I first heard the term *timber chicken* in reference to grouse. In a way he looks at the birds on his land like some sort of free-range game, with me as the harvester or the picture window if need be. Like the potatoes from his garden, the firewood from his maples, and the solar energy from the sun, grouse are just one more blessing from his land. And, fortunately for me, he's more than willing to share the wealth.

On Wildlife Art

I T WAS A TWO-HOUR APPOINTMENT with the dentist, who is a good friend and also an avid grouse hunter. His office is filled with wildlife prints, many of which depict grouse. This day, I was getting a broken molar repaired, along with a new crown. At times I wish I were like my dogs and could just ignore my aging teeth. They chew bones until their gums bleed, and a cracked tooth seems little more than an inconvenience.

While reclining in the dental chair, I watched a thunderstorm roll in, listened to the satellite radio, and contemplated the art hanging on the walls. One wall featured a winter wildlife scene: three grouse flushing in the December sun, birch and pine in the background. The sky was a deep blue, the snow sparkling, and the birds hung in the air like zeppelins. It never happens like that for me, I thought.

Back home later in the day, my mouth still numb, I was rereading a classic grouse text that featured wildlife art on its cover, a scene depicting again three birds flushing in the clear, one tilting away from the reader, offering a tempting shot at the vitals. In the background were birch, white pine, and flaming maples at the height of the fall color season.

In my study hangs another grouse scene, so I got up to have a look. It features just two grouse: one perched on what looks like a downed oak branch, the other flushing dead center in the picture, just hanging in the air, once again rather like a zeppelin. White birch trees stand in the background, along with what look to be spruce behind a hanging fog. It looks like early November, the leaves on the ground, the sun softened and low. The lighting in the picture seems true. The birds, however, look like they are stuffed, and I can't remember when I saw a grouse perched on a log twenty yards away, looking as if it didn't know death was stalking close by.

The picture was a gift from my brother-in-law, an Iowa pheasant hunter who has never swung a shotgun on grouse. He may think the cover in the picture is thick, which it would be to an Iowa pheasant hunter, but it's as good as it gets to a grouse or woodcock hunter. Still I enjoy the picture since it makes me think of grouse whenever I pass by.

Much of our wildlife art is highly romanticized, which is understandable for artists who want to sell their work. We won't buy pictures of a grouse getting its head blown off or a woodcock disintegrated by chokes too tight and loads too heavy. We won't buy pictures of hunting in a deluge or slogging through tag alder thickets that cut our hands and cheeks and poke and scratch our eyes. We don't want pictures of the birds that flashed as dim silhouettes through the popples or those that flushed unseen. How does one paint what one hasn't seen anyway?

If I were a realistic wildlife artist, my paintings would show walls of dense popple, treacherous thickets of swampy tag alders, logging roads choked with blackberries and impenetrable thorn apple hedges. The birds would fly at crazy and unexpected angles, and the hunters would often miss. The dog would bust birds, and the hunters would yell and curse at the dog. The sky would hang gray and heavy, the weather turning ugly—windy and sleety. The hunters would trip, fall, and bash their shotguns on trees and granite. The dogs would get deer ticks, lacerated feet, and bloody ears. And I would not sell a single painting.

We want the romantic version, not the bittersweet one, for that's what we'll plunk down $250 for or bid on at a Ruffed Grouse Society banquet. We want to be reminded of the way things ought to be or how we hope them to be. We want the sun to always shine, the dog to point every bird, and every shot to fly true to the mark. Idealists for the most part, we want to live in that always October when we are young, the dog fleet, and the woods teeming with grouse.

Empty Hulls

MY ENGLISH SETTER HOPPED out of the woods and onto the trail in front of me. His nose halfway to the ground, the dog turned and retreated back into the popple. I tensed my fingers around the fore end and trigger guard of my shotgun. Seconds passed, no bird flushed, and the dog reappeared, covering ground quickly. I loosened my grip and continued forward down the trail.

Every autumn, I return to this cover, even though it has matured well past its bird-holding prime and some of the aspens are now as thick as my waist. Still the place has special meaning for me, so I return every October for at least one annual visit. I shot one of my first grouse here with a singleshot 12-gauge the year Susan and I were married—at the time it was the only gun we owned and could afford. With its thirty-inch barrel and modified choke, it was decidedly not a classic grouse or woodcock gun. I bought it in high school with paper route money, and occasionally down through the years I hit a bird with it. Even though I shot that grouse almost twenty years ago and can still see it fall, to this day I'm shocked that I actually hit it and it fell.

Walking the same road years later, I carried a sleek gun, an English-stocked over-and-under, the kind of gun I dreamed about as a kid. It was a birthday gift from my wife, and, although I dearly love the gun and the thought behind the gun, I can't say that I enjoy the hunting any more now than when I was a kid shooting a used singleshot.

Back on the trail I reminisced about old guns and long-dead dogs and birds. A shotgun blasted behind us, down the trail back toward our truck parked at the gate, bringing me back to the world at hand. It sounded like a hunter was following us in. There was only one way into the woods, the logging road we were on, so whoever was behind us was coming in over our tracks. He or she had to know I was another hunter—the kennel in my truck, the Ruffed Grouse Society stickers, the half-empty box of shells on the dash. I was a bit peeved, an unjustified selfishness on my part. Even though we were on public land, I wanted the place to myself. I picked up my pace, hoping to put some distance between us. Five minutes after that first shot, a barrage erupted behind us. It began with two shots, then the semi-automatic salute—one, two, three, four, five shots in rapid succession, the first shell still in the air before the final is fired. I couldn't help but recite the five *M*s: one shot meat, two shots maybe, three shots miss, four shots moron, five shots might as well go home. I stepped up my pace again until we arrived at a large cutting, which we slipped into and headed due north bushwhacking toward the river a half mile distant.

We eventually outdistanced these hunters (I figured they had to be plural with all of the shooting), but now and again throughout the morning we heard them blazing away. Perhaps they were just target shooting, but the shots kept moving around, sometimes closer, sometimes farther away. With all the firing, they must have carried a couple of boxes of shells each into the woods. At one point I thought we had rid ourselves of their presence, and then they let go another barrage, sounding like it was a quarter mile away as the grouse flies. Despite their nagging presence, we had a good hunt that day. My notes about that day say we came home with a pair of grouse and three woodcock in a little over three hours of hunting.

A few hundred yards from my truck on the walk out, we came across five red shell casings scattered across the logging road, still smelling sweetly of gunpowder. The evidence of that first barrage, the semiautomatic salute. The 12-gauge shells were cheap game loads. They were loaded with #8 shot—not a bad choice for woodcock and grouse. I picked them up—a habit—and pocketed them. They weren't worth reloading, but they didn't belong there in the middle of the trail either.

I looked around for feathers, for any sign that these shells had brought down a bird. Circling with the dog around the brush off the logging road, I couldn't find any sign of a downed bird. But then I didn't really expect to find any, not after the semiautomatic salute, the reflex of an inexperienced hunter—or the occasional frustrated one.

Back at the gate an old Toyota pickup sat parked next to mine. Through the windshield, I could see the boxes that held the shells I had picked up. Two camouflage gun cases were flung on the bench seat. An uncontrollable urge came over me, and I lined up the five red shells on the driver's side wiper, then I pulled two empty shells out of my pocket, green Remington casings, and plucked a tail feather from each grouse and lined them up on the other wiper. Maybe they got the message: two shots, two birds. It was a smart-ass thing to do, but the urge was too strong.

I pick up spent shells in the field, not just mine but any I find. For one thing, I reload my own shells and sometimes hunters use high-quality casings worth recycling and reloading. It's a Depression era mentality instilled in me by my father, and I can still remember as a kid buying shells by the handful at the local hardware store because I couldn't afford a full box.

Shells also look trashy strewn around the woods. Sometimes hunters who shoot pumps or semiautos have a hard time recovering their casings, which go zinging out of the receiver after each shot, but doublegun shooters have no excuse for leaving casings behind. Mostly, though, I pick up shells because I like to unravel the stories they tell. Not finding shells is almost as revealing, too, since no shells could mean no birds.

In Wisconsin's grouse woods, I find a surprising number of #6 shell casings, which is the standard pheasant load in Iowa, a bird about three times the size of a grouse and about ten times as hard to kill. The #7½s outnumber the #6s slightly. Occasionally, I see #8s and almost never #9s, which is what I shoot, subscribing to the theory that more shot is better than larger and heavier shot. Burton Spiller wrote in his classic *Grouse Feathers* that he would use #10 shot when he could find it. That was seventy years ago. I have never seen #10 shot for sale, so I settle for #9.

After collecting empty casings for years, I conclude that a majority of Wisconsin hunters use 12-gauges, although I do see a fair number of yellow or green 20-gauge hulls. Every so often I come across a 16-gauge, and I almost never pick up a 28-gauge casing. I figure the hunters carrying these guns are pretty serious, not just guys out for a walk in the woods in hopes of getting a crack at something. These shells probably came from an over-and-under or a side-by-side, guns handed down from generation to generation, guns well cared for that are cleaned respectfully after each and every hunt.

An annual survey from the Loyal Order of Dedicated Grouse Hunters reveals how uncommon these off gauges are. In 2008, only four of sixty-one Wisconsin hunters who filled out the survey shot a 28-gauge and eleven carried 16-gauges. Among loyal and dedicated grouse hunters, the 20-gauge might be the most popular shotgun size, with nearly half (twenty-eight) of the sixty-one Wisconsin respondents using this gauge, mostly configured as doubleguns. Second most popular in the 2008 survey was the 12-gauge. Seventeen of the sixty-one respondents shot 12s, and again most were doubleguns. Despite these numbers, using my rather unscientific methods of just picking up shells, I'd estimate that the average Wisconsin grouse hunter, the guy who casually goes out a couple of times per year, shoots a 12-gauge and most likely he shoots #6 shot out of a pump or an autoloader, the same gun used on a duck or a pheasant hunt, perhaps even for deer hunting.

In the end, though, the gun or the load doesn't matter—being out in the woods is what counts. Killing birds shouldn't be the first priority of grouse and woodcock hunters. We hunt for other, less tangible reasons: a ramble in the autumn woods, the tang of crisp November air, or the sight of golden leaves sifting down to the ground. Along the way we collect memories and stories. And some people, like me, collect empty casings and the stories they leave behind.

New Wood

ON JULY 9, 1979, A TRUCK STRUCK and killed a wolf on a logging road in western Lincoln County, leading to a DNR investigation. The agency discovered that a wolf pack was living in this area, called New Wood by locals after the river that drains the area. This was a big deal because wolves were supposedly exterminated from Wisconsin decades earlier. Wildlife managers thought a few wolves roamed the woods of extreme northern Wisconsin, but New Wood was one hundred miles south of Lake Superior, far south of what wildlife biologists thought was the wolf's established range.

Today, the DNR's wolf pack distribution map shows five packs established in the adjacent area, including the South Averill Creek Pack, which is known for its depredations in the area. A few years back I saw a picture of a bear hound killed and eaten by New Wood wolves. Not much was left of the dog except a skeleton and a rear paw, and even though I know wolves can pounce on and kill a dog I continue to chance a wolf encounter and hunt there. The wolves have as much right as I do to roam and hunt the area, but still they make me feel a bit uneasy each time we come across scat, a reminder that we're not the only hunters in the area.

New Wood is both big enough and wild enough to support wolves, and rumors occasionally fly around about mountain lions there. Large black bears in the vicinity of five hundred pounds are taken each year in season, and fishers, bobcats, coyotes, and lesser predators all prowl about the thousands of acres of rolling woodland and northern swamp.

Several roads cut through New Wood, as well as miles of logging road and old railroad grades once used to haul virgin timber. I routinely happen across the old grades, long grown over with second-growth timber, which connected the numerous logging camps in the area: Natzke, Camp 6, Camp 25, Camp 26, Camp 27. From the camps the lumberjacks and teamsters worked with handsaws to cut what then was considered an infinite resource—the pineries of the north woods. When they pulled out and moved on, they left a sea of stumps and long views, the area looking like Nagasaki after the bomb.

But it wasn't long before the new second growth started, and this young and thriving habitat benefited much of the local wildlife: whitetail deer, bears, rabbits, and some species of songbirds, as well as woodcock and grouse. Scandinavian farmers followed the lumberjacks, grubbing stumps out of their rock-filled fields, but the poor soil, climate, and the cold did most of them in. Hunters bought out the farmers, throwing up makeshift cabins and camps, and today New Wood hunting land is difficult and expensive to buy. The county still cuts the New Wood country regularly, maintaining large tracts of aspen for pulpwood, and this indirectly benefits both grouse and woodcock, so in the fall I go there as often as possible, seeking these game birds.

New Wood covers several thousand acres, roughly the watershed drained by the New Wood River. Like the name suggests, New Wood has plenty of new wood, acres and acres of small aspen cuttings at various stages of succession, and the county continues to log it hard, making more bird cover. Some of the older cuttings are beyond maturity, the popple rotting and falling, clogging the ground, and making walking difficult. Blackberries thrive in the open spaces underneath these older trees, the canes shredding my pants, lacerating my boots, and bloodying my face and hands. My dogs slice their tongues and run with blood on their muzzles and chests, looking like their wild brothers lurking in the shadows. Occasionally we flush a bird in the older and overgrown sections that were prime years ago, but mainly I return for sentimental reasons, to remember dogs and birds from years past.

In New Wood, cuttings are always coming into their prime as grouse and woodcock cover. Just recently I was pleased to see that birds had returned to a cutting seven or eight years old. I'd shot birds in the aspen before it was cut, but it had overmatured as grouse cover and needed to be harvested. This popple upland slopes down to tag alders that border a pond, and there were predictably grouse up in the popple and woodcock down in the tags. Occasionally the two species mixed. Then the county harvested the section, and for several seasons I would hump through it on my way to productive cover, figuring it was yet too young and open to hold birds. The dog, however, recently corrected me and promptly wound himself into a tight point right off the trail in this now thriving head-high popple. I again figured incorrectly and guessed it was woodcock, moving just ahead of the dog, where woodcock often lie. Instead a grouse flushed, popping out on my left, leaving me to corkscrew around to try to catch up with it. I never did. But that first bird woke me up so I was ready for a second point, which came just beyond the first, and shot a large brown-phased grouse, pleased to see the cover productive once again. It was as though I had an old friend back.

New Wood wasn't always this way: new and thriving. Before the arrival of the lumber camps—industrious man with his sharp ax and crosscut saw—it was mostly virgin white pine, red oak, maple, and hemlock on the uplands, massive old growth in a primal forest. Balsam fir, spruce, and tag alder lined the lowlands. In the early years of the twentieth century, this part of Lincoln County was clear-cut thoroughly, just as the rest of the state was, and the logs were floated down the river, which joins the Wisconsin north of Merrill, the old narrow-gauge rail lines snaking through the woods to take the virgin timber to the river. Today the grades are level places to walk while hunting. Here and there I run across old stumps rotting and molding back into the rocky soil, some of them well over three feet in diameter, a grim reminder of the two-hundred-foot white pines that once swayed here. The piles of lumber at the sawmills must have been immense—a sight worth seeing.

In the 1960s, a new threat emerged. Part of New Wood was nearly submerged when the Army Corp of Engineers proposed building a dam that would have flooded over two thousand acres, drowning out the many rapids along the river, as well as some prime fishing spots. A group calling itself the New Wood Society was formed, a coalition of fly fisherman, hunters, hikers, and environmentalists, to protest the proposed dam. Tramping through the area, I often think of how lucky we are to have this place and thank the New Wood Society for standing up to the folly of building a dam here.

As much as I love big trees—there are still some growing along the river—it's the new wood that produces and holds the birds, the acres and acres of aspen, called popple around here. Tag alder, hazelnut, balsam fir, dogwood, and thorn apple add to the mix, creating classic Wisconsin grouse cover. As much as I appreciate the old growth, the new growth engenders an explosion of new life, both plant and animal.

Yet even if New Wood weren't ideal cover, I'd still be up here wandering around on an autumn afternoon because the place is like an old comfortable sweatshirt. I don't often pull out my compass here, but instead orient myself by old familiar landmarks: a crumbling stone foundation, an S-shaped cherry tree, the yellow blazes of the Ice Age Trail, the corner where I shot my first Wisconsin grouse so many years ago, now growing into sugar maples. The county has yet to log this corner and bring the birds back, but I hunt it every year in the hope that someday a bird will flush from the same spot. I can still see the two birds that flushed here almost twenty years ago. They vaulted into the sky, and yet somehow I managed to hit one, bringing to earth a bird that would forever change my life.

One particular day a few years ago I needed the comfort of New Wood. We had just received a letter from the city of Wausau informing us that it intended to build a four-lane road right through the middle of our house—in the front door, through the living room and bathroom, and out the garage. When I opened the letter walking back from the mailbox, I nearly collapsed in the driveway. Our life teetered for a while after that, and shortly thereafter I drove up to New Wood hoping for some answers. I wanted to sit on my favorite rock underneath the massive white pines that stand sentinel along the river, the dog lying at my feet impatient to get on, and listen to the river tumble over granite boulders. I hoped the broad sweep of the October sky, lit by maples on a far ridge, would quiet my fear. I needed to know there was a place still big enough for wolves and bears and a hunter who was willing to walk back into big country.

Months later we learned that the city planned to move its four-lane road seventy-five yards to the east, sparing our house but taking the neighbor's. Today the road runs over and down what was once known as Woods's Hill and right by our house. The months of construction wore us out. At daybreak we'd be greeted with the piercing nag of backup beepers on earthmovers and dump trucks, the squeal of rusty tracks on Caterpillars, and the roar of diesel engines in the massive backhoes. It was if someone were endlessly dragging fingernails over a chalkboard. A line from a Gary Snyder poem played an endless loop through my mind: "The pain of the work of wrecking the world." The chickadees, nuthatches, indigo buntings, and wood thrushes fled, and it felt like the sky was falling.

Where our home sits on this north-sloping hill was never prime bird habitat, the trees too mature, the soil too rocky, and hemlock and yellow birch dominating the ecosystem. Even so, an occasional grouse wandered through, and the April before the construction a half dozen woodcock performed their sky dance in the overgrown field across from our house. Today most of this wooded cover is gone, and a local developer has scheduled the rest to be razed next year for a luxury home development. The deer and turkeys, their home clear-cut, now wander through our yard, looking for whatever cover and food they can scrounge.

We can see what is to come. This new road will become one of the busiest in the city, and development will follow the road—strip malls, big-box and convenience stores, acres of pavement, overhead lights, and stoplight trees. The city might finally get that Red Lobster or Olive Garden it's been clamoring for. We don't share the city leaders' progressive dream, which for us has turned into a nightmare, preferring wild country to pavement, grouse and woodcock to the bright lights and noisy desperation of our consumer culture.

At that time I needed a sense of place, and New Wood gave it to me. Like the deer and turkeys that development displaced, we, too, will be displaced someday, a cost of progress, and right now it's easy for us to see our plight connected to the neighborhood habitat and wildlife. In the end we are all animals who require food, shelter, clothing, and fuel, just as the chickadees and squirrels do, something humans often forget. We can't eat neon lights and plastic. Year by year we lose a bit more of our connection to the earth. We forget that rocks, trees, plants, and animals nurture us, not the world of concrete, steel, and plastic we have manufactured.

This is why I come to New Wood—to remember my connection to the earth. Yet in the back of my mind I know that even New Wood won't be safe forever. The wolves could once again vanish, this time perhaps never to return. We're all just one bad decision away from obliteration.

Sauntering Along

GOOD QUALITY BOOTS ARE VITAL for the grouse hunter. Roughly calculated, I walk about two miles for every grouse bagged. Expending more calories hunting the bird than I gain eating it, I realize a net caloric loss, which would be catastrophic for a wolf or an owl. Unlike the wolf or the owl, we do not survive by hunting alone, which is a good thing since nearly all modern people, myself included, would starve if this were the case. At any rate, during the hunting season, I walk in the woods more than at any other time of the year through places I wouldn't go if not hunting.

Like Thoreau, another great walker, I am a self-appointed surveyor of popple slashings and tag alder thickets, doing my duty faithfully each autumn. I have inspected logging roads and forest paths and rambled cross-country with compass in hand, wearing holes in my boots and tearing my pants literally to threads, even double-thickness brush pants. For my labor and pains, the miles of trekking over rough country, and the slashes of unfriendly brush, I have received great rewards. Besides the birds we've eaten, I have come home laden with treasures, both material and immaterial. The woods are full of riches: deer antlers, bird nests, feathers, plants to identify, things to stuff in my game bag, which can hold more than dead birds. Besides the tangible I'm also rewarded with the intangible—a fisher treed by the dog, hundreds of mallards simultaneously flushing from a lonesome pond, wolf tracks, stories for later.

I prefer pointing dogs to flushing dogs or no dog at all because they let me saunter through the woods, my mind going where it will as I travel along. With a flushing dog or no dog, a hunter needs to be keyed up always, tensed and ready to fire at the sudden flush of a grouse. With a pointing dog ahead, I can simply follow along as he does the work of finding and holding birds. Several times per season as I'm dreaming an afternoon away, I lose the dog for a spell, my sub-conscious finally registering the piercing utter quiet—the silence after the constant tinkling of the dog's bell. Meanwhile the dog is rigid, staring down a bird somewhere in the brush and waiting for me to take notice.

Most times it takes me just a few minutes to locate the dog, usu-ally pointing a woodcock, but there have been times when it took much longer. A few times I've resorted to firing my shotgun over-head, hoping the dog would report to the sound of the gun, and once it took two shots to find the dog. When all I heard after that second shot was the wind high up in the trees, my mind quickly jumped to the worst-case scenario, the dog gone forever, me the irresponsible owner. But then I heard the faint tinkle of the dog's bell, a mere thirty yards away, pointing a woodcock. He had held staunchly through all my whistling, hollering, and shotgun blasts. I walked over, flushed the bird, then gave him a bear hug. He tolerated the hug but clearly wanted to continue the hunt.

Saunter is an ancient word, and lexicographers speculate that it comes down to us from *Sainte Terre*, as in "holy terrain." Later it came to mean the unhurried pace of pilgrims in the Middle Ages bound for the Holy Land. It's an apt word for the grouse hunter who sets forth on a pilgrimage to seek the holy places: an ancient red oak in the midst of a sea of popple; thorn apples alongside a sagging barbed wire fence, creeping into what was once pasture; a crumbling granite foundation, all that's left of a Swedish settler's hope to farm a cold and harsh land.

Maybe *holy* is too strong a word for some, a reference to the sacred groves considered blasphemous by the Old Testament. Regardless, to some the woods hold special places (power vortexes a friend calls them), a stark contrast to the urban spaces we have built over the top of these wild lands. That two hundred years ago Milwaukee and Chicago were beautiful, wild places is hard to grasp. We cut down, tear up, and pave over for one more strip mall or housing development, replacing what Leopold called "natural, wild and free" with places unnatural, tame, and stale.

When I set forth on a hunt, I might plan to return to my truck by noon, perhaps later, but always before nightfall, unlike the Sainte Terres, who left the security of home, the comfort of family, the sweetness of friends, and the regularity of work. They gave up all, begging as they shuffled south in search of the Holy Land. Ivan Turgenev's Russian narrator in his *Sketches from a Hunter's Album* did the same, wandering through the steppes, sleeping wherever he happened to find himself: with peasants out in the open alongside a river, in a forester's hovel, or every once in a while in the comfort of some nobleman's manor house.

The pilgrim mind-set was more singular than mine, which gets cluttered while in the field with problems from home and work. Henry David Thoreau had the same problem. "I am alarmed when it happens that I have walked a mile in the woods bodily, without getting there in spirit," he wrote. "In my afternoon walk I would fain forget all my morning occupations and my obligations to society. But it sometimes happens that I cannot easily shake off the village." Once, while breaking for lunch on a high point, the friend hunting with me pulled out his cell phone and called his workplace, just checking in, he said in apology. I wanted to grab his phone, throw it in the air, and blast it to pieces with #9 shot like a clay pigeon. He noticed my stare, explaining that he always carried his cell phone in the woods in case he got lost or just wanted to speak to his wife. "It's got GPS, too," he crowed. Battery-powered wisdom in a plastic case is more like it, I thought.

Sometimes it takes me a mile or so to lose myself in the woods, to shake off the city in my case. Unlike a dog, my entry into the wild is not immediate and complete. It takes me some time to rid myself of the dust and clamor of urbanization. Often the dog's first point frees me from our modern world and hauls me back to a much older one. Perhaps a wild flush, one right under my feet or from a branch overhead, will shake me awake. Or maybe the unique shape of a cloud on the horizon will make me forget about a stack of papers I need to grade or an expensive car repair. Sooner or later I get into the saun- tering mind-set on most hunts, although I have cut hunts short and turned around early. The world is sometimes too much with us, even in the most desolate of places.

Sauntering through the woods is good for our health, both phys- ical and mental. Thoreau claimed that he needed at least four hours a day spent "sauntering through the woods and over the hills and fields" to preserve his health. He went on to write that he couldn't believe shopkeepers and factory workers who spent all their daylight hours inside toiling hadn't yet committed suicide. Thoreau claimed he needed to get outside everyday so he wouldn't "acquire some rust." Come autumn I pine for the woods, drawn by the season of slanting light and rarified autumn air, to wear off my rust.

Sometimes sauntering forth and leaving the city behind, along with work and responsibility, causes problems. Unlike Thoreau, I am married, and even though Susan expects little from me around the house this time of year, we usually have our yearly row over raking the leaves in our yard. Unfortunately, our house is surrounded by 150-year-old oaks and maples, which drop a million or so leaves, annually coinciding with the best bird hunting of the season. There is frost nearly every morning, moving ducks and geese and eventually the woodcock south. Every October I tell her we should hire the raking out, but we don't, so I drag a few tarp loads into the woods behind the house until October's siren song seduces me and I steal away. I can't help myself. I beg Susan to come with me, we'll pay some neighbor kid to finish the raking, but the story always ends the same—me raking halfheartedly until I can't stand to do so any longer and Susan the responsible homeowner.

My other relationships suffer as well. People are forever asking me to do things in the fall. Relatives want us to drive south and visit for the weekend. I've skipped out on weddings and birthday celebrations, but in my defense there are only four weekends in October. If I could quit my job in October, I would, especially since I feel like I have more important work to do, sauntering around the woods counting the falling leaves and passing geese overhead. And with a little luck, maybe I'll shoot a grouse or two.

The Mythical Bird

WE WERE TRUDGING BACK toward my truck after a long, slow day of hunting on state-owned land in Langlade County. Grouse were at the bottom of their cycle that year, and we had not seen a bird all morning after four hours of hunting and miles of walking. In a good year when grouse are at the peak of their cycle, I would encounter as many as two dozen birds in the land we had just covered. I have hunted this area for years, dozens of times, and walking the familiar logging roads and trails I saw the points, flushes, and shots of all the preceding autumns. In my mind birds flushed in astonishing numbers, the years layered over each other like the lacquer on a fine piece of furniture.

When we got back to the parking lot, we ran into a DNR biologist. He asked how we did, looking at my empty game bag. I told him we got skunked.

"Did you see any?"

"Not a one. Zippo. Nada."

"It sure is a bad year," he said, petting the dog. "He looks like he had fun, though."

"He always does, birds or no birds."

Unlike the dog, I need at least one bird to keep me going. Faith, belief, hope, call it what you will, but I will hike for two or three hours knowing a grouse lies at the end of the trek. It's not that I need to kill something to leave the woods satisfied, because in the peak years I have come home empty-handed due to my inept shooting, poor dog work, or sometimes just plain bad luck. Sometimes the birds just don't cooperate, which is good for them. That morning in Langlade County, though, it felt as though we were hunting in a desert. Where were all the birds? What causes them to die off so suddenly? And most important, would they come back? I couldn't imagine or face an October without a ruffed grouse flushing, a sound so distinct once heard.

That day, and others like it, gave rise to the phrase "the mythical bird," which is that one last bird you wish you would see before quitting for the day. *Webster's* first definition of *mythical* concerns something that exists in mythology, like the phoenix rising from the ashes; Raven, so prevalent in Native American stories; or Hugin and Munin, the ravens that serve as Odin's spies in Norse mythology. The mythical bird I'm referring to corresponds to the second definition, the bird imagined or invented. It's the bird willed into existence at the end of a long day when grouse seem as scarce as woodcock teeth or when a hunter can't seem to hit a pumpkin in a tree ten yards away and wants just one more chance. The mythical bird by definition comes at the end of a hunt, at times when the shotgun is unloaded and cased and the dog kenneled. It materializes just when I have stopped hunting and am beginning to think of things other than the hunt.

Most days the mythical bird remains mythical, but occasionally one materializes out of thin air, or thin cover as it were, and this occurs often enough to keep the hope simmering that I can mentally produce such a thing just by wishing for it. When it happens I feel like I could levitate or change stones into gold. In reality it's all blind luck, the happenstance of two lines intersecting: that of the hunter and that of the grouse. If I happen to shoot a grouse, the serendipity is all mine. For the mythical bird, the grouse at the wrong place at the wrong time, it's bad karma, fat chance, destiny.

Usually I wish for the mythical bird in the lean years, when the birds are at the bottom of the cycle or I haven't seen a bird for hours, and I want to remember the thrill of a flush or just know ruffed grouse still exist. But the mythical bird just happens. Like any flush, it's beyond our control. Occasionally, though, the mythical bird crops up on a day when birds are plentiful, when he's welcome but not really necessary. The last one I remember occurred recently during a year of plentiful grouse. I was hunting Ox that day, and he was nearly flawless, pointing birds that were holding until I walked in for the flush. They held tightly and flushed in dependable and unswerving trajectories. On such days the birds slow down, and it's as if I can see every feather on their bodies when they flush.

By the end of the morning, I had shot four birds, and my game bag was getting comfortably heavy, the birds still warm against my back. I smiled thinking of the dishes these birds would make—curried grouse, grilled grouse, grouse pie. The freezer was empty back home. With the truck nearly in my sight just over the last hill, a grouse scooted across the trail into a young popple cutting. I called Ox to my side, made him heel, and quickly approached the spot where the bird went into the brush. Ox wheeled around on the trail when he hit the scent cone and crept a few yards into the woods, flash pointing, point following quick point. I stood on the trail, keyed up for the shot, but it never came. For several minutes Ox worked over the cover, pointing here and there but always moving on, the sign of a bird running.

He was forging ahead deeper into the woods, so I reluctantly followed. I was tired, had four birds already, and didn't want to be a game hog. (The daily limit is five.) We worked across the hillside and down the slope. Then we came back up the hillside. In short we went over what seemed like every foot of that cover, every possible place the bird could have been, until I started to think a make-believe bird had sprinted across the trail. It really was a mythical bird. I called Ox over, and we made our way back to the trail, returning to the very spot where I thought the bird had crossed.

We were within a few yards of the trail still in the popple when Ox pointed in front of a brush pile. I didn't believe him, thinking he was getting old scent. I called to him. "No bird, Oxie. There's no bird. He's long gone." He wouldn't move, so I just stood there with him. We stayed that way for a couple of minutes, and when I reached down to grab him to pull him out to the trail so we could go home a bird flushed out of that brush pile. Instinctively, I let go of his collar and shouldered my gun. Since the trees were young, about as thick as pool cues and about ten feet high, I had a clear shot. The bird crumpled, and Ox retrieved our fifth bird of the day. That was Ox's eleventh hunting season and the last time we would limit and get five birds in one day, one of the reasons I shot a fifth bird. As I sat there smoothing feathers on the bird and admiring the large gray fan, I remembered a day long ago on this very same trail, down the hill about one hundred yards to the north.

I was walking out of the woods with an empty game bag. In a funk, I was thinking about something other than grouse hunting when I noticed the dog was missing, his bell no longer ringing. I turned to my left, and there he was just a few yards off the trail on point. I stopped and stared momentarily, the impact of the point not immediately registering on my foggy brain. Then habit took over, and I waded into the woods off the trail, down a slight depression, up to a blowdown bordering tag alders not more than twenty yards from the trail. Suddenly, the bird popped out behind me, almost back at the trail. It flew into the clear out over the trail and headed back up the ridge we had just walked down. It should have been an easy shot, but as I spun around my feet got tangled in the brush and I stumbled. In short, I missed with both barrels, firing above and behind the bird into a background of balsams, cleanly missing the mythical bird, the best chance of the day.

I dragged myself the last quarter mile to my truck wondering how I could miss such an easy shot. How could I hit some shots that seemed impossible and miss one of the easiest of the season? Maybe I just imagined that one. Gunnar seemed to think not, the scent of the bird still fresh in his mind. Dogs, ever hopeful, always believe in the mythical bird. They think there's always one more just over the next ridge, never for a moment losing their faith.

Soul Food

WE HAD WALKED THE MILE OR SO from our cabin to Martel's Pothole, a glacial depression dug out during the last ice age. In southern Wisconsin these landforms are called kettles; in northern Wisconsin they're called frost pockets. Martel's had been logged a few years earlier, and all of the new growth shooting up made for prime grouse habitat. We routinely ride our mountain bikes through here, and just about every time, we scare up a bird or two, so we thought the long hike to Martel's for a hunt well worth the effort.

We arrived, and in short order Ox went on point. While we searched for the dog in the thick aspen, an ATV puttered toward us. We couldn't see the machine through the trees and brush, but it was definitely moving down the trail toward us. Suddenly it stopped, and the rider killed the motor. It was still for a few seconds until a loud BOOM shattered the quiet of the woods. The shot ripped through the brush not far from us and even closer to Ox.

The ATVer had stopped, pulled out his shotgun, and blasted the bird on the ground Ox was pointing. My dog was probably within ten yards of the bird, although to be fair to the ATVer he had no idea that we were there. Fortunately, Ox didn't get sprayed with #6 or #8 shot. When we got to him, he was mouthing the bird, and we could see where the shot had ripped up the ground nearby, shredding brush and scattering feathers. From this it was clear that the ATVer had ground swatted the bird, offering it little if any fair chance.

The guy rolled up to us, and I commanded Ox to drop the bird. He did so, and it lay there in the dust and leaves at his feet. I refused to hand the bird to the sportsman and called Ox over. He could get off his contraption and pick it up himself. He wanted to chat, but I was in no mood to do so after he had nearly shot my dog. I was hot, held a 12-gauge, and at that moment really felt like shooting out his tires. On the other hand, the ATVer was within his legal rights riding in this section of the county forest, as well as ground swatting a sitting bird. The DNR prohibited neither.

Later, as we walked home under the low gray sky of a perfectly ruined October day, Susan reminded me that I had no right to criticize and then played devil's advocate for the sportsman. "Maybe he needed it for food." I reminded her that he was driving a five-thousand-dollar ATV and could probably afford chicken. "Yes, but he still might be hungry." After a bit she asked, "So what makes your way of killing them any better?" She had a point. Dead was dead, and hunting ethics didn't matter to a dead grouse riding in an ice cream bucket strapped on the back of an ATV or riding in the pouch of my game bag.

Out in the woods there are no referees, no umpires or judges sitting high in the gallery checking to make sure that we play within the rules. What happens out in the upland and alder runs occurs simply between us and the grouse and the woodcock, with only the trees and the sky overhead bearing witness to the things we do, whether good or evil. No one is holding a gun to our heads and telling us how to behave. We can shoot birds on the ground, out of trees, or on the wing because in the field hunters individually must establish and adhere to their own ethics. The DNR has established daily bag and possession limits, as well as seasons and hunting hours, and hunter safety courses go beyond this, teaching the rules for handling firearms, marksmanship, and a more evolved hunting ethic like fair chase, but ultimately the individual hunter alone in the field must make his or her decisions about how to act.

Leopold's land ethic remains a solid starting point for developing a hunting ethic. Leopold, himself a hunter, wanted to extend ethical treatment to the land, treating it as part of the community rather than merely property to be bought and sold, ravaged and destroyed. Instead of dominating nature—the land, the soil, the plants and animals—he felt we should become part of it and treat it as we would like to be treated.

For one thing this means hunters limit the use of technology. We can, with modern technology, throw the balance between predator and prey so much in our favor that the prey has no chance whatsoever. Grouse, for some reason, don't fear motor vehicles. My wife works with a guy who regularly has a grouse fly up on his ATV and ride around his farm with him, occasionally on the top of his head.

On the other hand, they flee from four- and two-footed predators, a flight reaction deep in their genes. Many sportsmen know this and cruise slowly up and down fire and logging roads on ATVs and in trucks, their eyes straining for the silhouette of a foolhardy bird in the right-of-way. In many instances a driver can pull right up, roll down the window, and pot a reckless bird clucking around yards away. Old-timers have shown me their sawed-off .410s or 20-gauges with sly and conspiratorial looks, usually singleshots easy to conceal, as well as wield, in the confines of the interior of a truck or car. (Shooting a bird from inside a vehicle is prohibited by the DNR, as is discharging a firearm from a road on the Wisconsin Department of Transportation map.) This technique has many names—ground swatting, ground sluicing, Arkansasing. The last term is clearly unfair to Arkansas since in the case of the ATVer who nearly shot my dog, I could have written that he really "Wisconsined" that bird.

Then again, many antihunters would object not only to the ATVers' use of technology but also to my more limited use of technology. They could argue that my shotgun gives me an unfair advantage over grouse and woodcock or that it's nearly impossible to miss a bird pointed by a dog. Some see little difference between my mode of hunting and ground swatting, the effect of both the same in the end—a dead bird. Fair chase means little to a person who sees the taking of any animal life as murder, blood being blood by whatever means it was shed.

I struggle for an answer. I could not catch a grouse with my bare hands or in my teeth with the rare exception of a sick or crazy bird. I possess neither claws nor fangs and compared to wild animals move slowly; only my intellect and the weapons the intellect of other humans made give me the tools that allow me to kill grouse and woodcock. Without a shotgun in my hands, a healthy bird would evade me every time. It would also evade my dogs just about as readily. In order to kill a grouse consistently, we have to work together, me with a shotgun and the dog with its nose. Does my shotgun give me an unfair advantage? With no one looking on to judge us, that's a question hunters should ask.

Knowing all this and struggling with these questions, I still continue to go afield every autumn. I won't deny that I hunt for the sport, for the thrill of watching my dogs do their job and of a well-placed shot, but for me it goes beyond that. I don't want to eat meat from the supermarket, nor do I want someone else to do my killing. Like my dogs, I remain an unrepentant carnivore. Thoreau believed that as a boy matured he would outgrow hunting and not desire to "wantonly murder any creature, which holds its life by the same tenure that he does." He thought it natural for a young boy to grow up hunting and felt it was a fine introduction to the woods, but "if he has the seeds of a better life within him, he distinguishes his proper objects, as a poet or a naturalist it may be, and leaves the gun and fish-pole behind." I often wonder, though, whether or not Thoreau ate meat in his later years and if he really thought that obtaining meat was murder. In *Walden* he ate a woodchuck, as well as fish, and he wrote, "I could sometimes eat a rat with a good relish, if it were necessary." He sounds as conflicted as I sometimes am. The Spanish philosopher José Ortega y Gasset wrote that we combine the two extremes of mammals—herbivore and carnivore. Omnivores, we vacillate between being cows and wolves, which may explain our sometimes bewildering feelings about meat.

My desire to kill has waned over the years, and I don't pull the trigger with the same relish I did as a boy. Death is something I think about often in the field as the leaves sift to the ground around me, especially after losing two dogs in less than six months, a reminder of what's to come to all of us someday. Yet I still enjoy the taste of grouse and woodcock flesh and understand its benefits to my soul, clarifying as it does my position in the food chain. Leopold felt that hunting spelled out our "dependency on the soil-plant-animal-man food chain, and of the fundamental organization of the biota." When cleaning an animal, pulling the viscera out of a grouse or woodcock, it's dead clear to me that meat doesn't just magically appear shrink-wrapped in a supermarket cooler.

In Thoreau's opinion I may still be just a boy and in Ortega's philosophical wanderings only a confused mammal. But when I sink my teeth into the sweet, white flesh of grouse or the liverish meat of woodcock, I don't have regrets. Sitting down to a meal of wild game, I don't agonize about that I'm eating and fixate on the death of an innocent animal. Mostly I'm just thankful.

Shooting and Eating Locally

AS THE SMOKE CURLED OUT of the grill's vent holes, I got up, beer in hand, and walked across the patio and into the sweet-smelling odor—ruffed grouse basted in butter, thyme, and crushed garlic. I stood there and let the fragrance seep into my flannel shirt. A quietly beautiful October evening, it was still warm enough to grill outside. Most of the leaves were off the oak, ash, and maple trees and scattered about our yard. Soon we would do all our cooking indoors, chased inside by snow and cold.

That evening we had two breasts on the grill, birds from the previous autumn as we ate up birds from last year, optimistic we would replace them over the course of the new season. Most birds I freeze with water in Ziploc bags, big blocks of ice requiring extra room in the deep freeze, but they keep for years frozen this way. We've eaten meat five years old, forgotten birds crammed into a dark corner, and the flesh tasted no different than that of a bird frozen for a few weeks. We also eat freshly killed birds during the hunting season, but freezing a few each year allows us to enjoy their taste and sustenance year-round.

Earlier in the day, I foraged in the freezer and finally pulled out a bag labeled "2G '07 Nine Mile Skinny Cover." I write four things on the Ziploc bag—number and type of bird, year, and a place—so this block held two grouse shot in 2007 at a place I call the Skinny Cover. To me this is a special place, like all good covers—a place where the trail runs through the midst of a popple cutting, which thins into a marsh. Where I shot these birds, the strip of trees was no more than twenty yards wide. Writing the year and cover on the bag helps me relive the day, and a year later I could still see Ox pointing the birds, the feathering on his legs and tail wavering in the slight morning breeze. He pointed each bird individually, about five minutes apart. The dead and withered grass concealing the birds was rimed with frost, and when flushed both birds bolted out across the marsh, offering nearly identical and relatively easy shots in the thinning trees. It was morning, the sun low in the southeastern sky, the air glowing. Almost a year later the feathers still drifted lazily back to earth in this glow, the aroma of gunpowder mixing with pleasing smells wafting from the grill.

After five minutes a side, the birds were done, so I slid them off the grill and onto a plate. Served with wild rice and a cranberry sauce made from locally grown berries, the birds were the center of our October meal. To write that grouse tastes like chicken is a cliché, but that's how I explain its taste to those not familiar with the bird. Actually, grouse tastes more like the denser meat of a free-range chicken than an industrial chicken. To upland hunters, I would say it tastes like pheasant or quail, recognizing subtle differences among the three birds. Pheasant is tougher, drier, and wilder tasting, although each bird has at least twice as much meat as a grouse; to me quail have a blander taste than grouse, and the bird is so small (about the size of a robin) that it takes several to make a meal. Besides, for me to hunt either of these prairie-loving birds with any success I would have to drive several hundred miles to the southwest. Ruffed grouse and woodcock live in our neighborhood, so that's what we shoot and eat.

That said, however, I enjoy eating ruffed grouse more than any other game bird, and one reason we hunt them, among the many, is so we can eat them. Since ruffed grouse don't do well in captivity, resisting domestication and commercialization, and market hunting was banned nearly a century ago in Wisconsin, hunting remains the only reliable way to ensure a supply. Begging a good friend who hunts grouse or hoping one flies into the picture window or into a moving vehicle might yield a bird or two every now and then, but eating ruffed grouse with any regularity implies hunting ruffed grouse.

If I could avoid store-bought meat and eat just wild game, I would, but hunting and eating only wild game isn't really a sustainable proposition. First of all, if every Wisconsin resident ate one grouse per year, the population of birds would be decimated if not wiped out. At the peak of the last cycle (1999), the Wisconsin DNR estimated that hunters killed 768,000 birds, and that same year the U.S. Census Bureau ball-parked the state's population at 5.2 million people, which is roughly one bird for every seven residents. Even the state's 1.7 million deer (the estimated population before the 2008 gun deer season) couldn't feed the state. Buying domesticated beef, pork, and fowl is clearly more sustainable, at least in terms of viable game populations and feeding the state of Wisconsin.

Hunting grouse on a personal level doesn't make much economic or ecological sense either. I have never calculated my per-grouse costs—fuel, dogs and their associated costs, guns and ammunition (although many years I fire so few shells that the ammunition costs are negligible), hunting clothes, accessories, and license fees. They all add up, significantly. Grouse flesh is probably the most expensive meat we eat in our home looked at from a dollars-and-cents perspective.

It doesn't make ecological sense either to drive hundreds of miles through the season over several counties in pursuit of good cover, burning up nonrenewable resources and spewing carbon into the atmosphere. I hike several miles per bird bagged, expending more calories than those to be had from a single grouse. My dogs eat pounds of food every month so they will be fit and healthy enough to hunt with us, and they rarely get to taste grouse or use its calories. The calories we expend per bird runs into the thousands, even tens of thousands (a gallon of gas has roughly thirty thousand calories). It would make much more economic and ecological sense to raise free-range chickens in our backyard.

Then why hunt, kill, and eat grouse? As I wrote earlier, I enjoy the taste of grouse, and hunting them is the only reliable way to obtain them. In short, I hunt for self-indulgent and epicurean reasons. Grouse can't be bought in a store, so I must go and get them, which is fine with me for I know I'm getting natural protein not laced with antibiotics and fed with chemical-bathed feed. In that sense ruffed grouse are the ultimate in organic, free-range poultry.

Hunting also makes us at least a tad self-reliant. Like making raspberry jam from our berries, salsa from our tomatoes and cilantro, syrup from our maple trees, or firewood from our oaks and ash, hunting grouse is a way of providing for ourselves—gathering food rather than purchasing it from the supermarket. Hunting, gathering, and harvesting these goods may be a small part of my life, but I think it's important to rely on myself for at least some things. I like to be as little hooked to the corporations supplying us with our food and energy as possible. We may be fooling ourselves into thinking we are independent, especially since much of the rest of our meals when we serve grouse—the butter, garlic, rice, the beer, and wine—comes from the store and the food industry, yet even so it seems a step in the right direction, a much better option than a Chicken McNugget.

If Susan and I want to eat meat, doing our own killing, cleaning, and cooking of that meat seems an honest approach in a culture where most of the killing is done for us behind walls in factories so we remain willfully ignorant of the killing, as is the case with the McNugget. Many of us would eat less meat if we had to do our own killing, cleaning, and butchering. While grouse hunting I participate directly in the food chains, as Aldo Leopold explained in his "Land Ethic" section of *A Sand County Almanac*, describing these chains also as circuits and pyramids, the energy flowing from the broad base of the soil, the foundation of the pyramid, to the tip of the triangle where a few lone carnivores reside. In the case of ruffed grouse, Wisconsin soil nurtures the popple, dogwood, and tag alder, which produce the catkins and berries feeding the bird, which in turn feeds me. With woodcock, worms grow and thrive in the moist soils of seeps and bogs, where woodcock feed voraciously on them, developing the bird, which then feeds me. "Land, then, is not merely soil," wrote

Leopold. "It is a fountain of energy flowing through a circuit of soils, plants, and animals." Land is not just dirt, the hard stuff below our feet or a place to stick up a for sale sign. It is our very life, something most consumers have forgotten.

Knowing this, I no longer look at the woods and a dead grouse in hand the same way I look at chicken breasts in the frozen meat section. I don't want my food chain mediated for me at every meal. I want a meaningful relationship with the land; otherwise land becomes, as Leopold might have noted in contemporary terms, the space between cities on which McNuggets grow. Shooting and eating grouse grants me a sustaining and substantial connection to the land—if only a few times each year.

Acres of Goods

STROLLING UP AND DOWN THE AISLES, I was amazed at the number, variety, and complexity of the goods on sale. The floor space of this national hunting and fishing retailer spanned several acres, the square footage larger than a few of the grouse and woodcock coverts we hunt. Tree stands towered over aisle 3, the most expensive one looking a bit like the guard tower in the old *F Troop* TV series. Stacked next to the stands were deer scents, deer feed, antler supplements, and grunt calls. In the home section, the store offered camouflage recliners and sofas, useful in case one needs to hide the furniture. In aisle 8 the hunting clothing was mostly high-tech stuff: Gore-Tex as well as windproof, made from the latest synthetic and petroleum fabrics. Bright and menacing, the ATVs squatted in one corner of the store—a hunter doesn't even have to walk in the woods anymore.

In aisle 10 I found what I needed among the dog beds, retrieving dummies, and beeper and shock collars—a simple bell for the dog, Swiss made, $6.95. After years of hard use, my bell had broken, the

clapper falling out somewhere in the woods on a hunt. Ox had literally run that bell into the ground. Our dogs wear a bell so we can tell
their whereabouts in the thick woods, and when it goes silent for
several seconds it usually means the dog is on point somewhere in
the brush and we must find him quickly. I grabbed a bell and headed
back toward the cashiers somewhere to the north, hoping I didn't
need a compass to find my way there.

"You find everything you needed?"

"Yes, and then some." Like a Mossy Oak Break-Up sofa and a
camouflage bikini, I thought.

"MasterCard or Visa?"

I slapped a ten-dollar bill down on the counter.

The hunting industry in Wisconsin, like those in many states, is
a billion-dollar industry, employing thousands of workers and stim-
ulating the economy in ways that would surprise even Adam Smith.
American hunters are fond of buying gadgets to give them an edge in
the field, and whether we admit it or not, most of us like to buy stuff.
Some men might not admit this, but we do like to go shopping—at
least on our terms and in the place of our choosing. Our gadgets do
help us, and yet many of us do not question the unfair edge the technology we employ produces or how it might throw off the balance
between predator and prey so that hunting might no longer be hunting. In some cases hunting has become merely shooting; in extreme
cases it is not even that. When the odds have been tipped so greatly
in our favor, the contest is no longer a contest, for we have passed the
boundary between fair chase and slaughter. One of the greatest
threats to hunting today is making it too effortless and undemanding.

Hunting should require effort, placing demands on our intellects and bodies.

Grouse and woodcock hunters, like anyone else, are not immune to the lure of high-tech gadgets. We are seduced by the doodads the business world has manufactured. With GPS we can navigate through the woods with relative ease, and a hunter can mark the exact locations of the birds flushed and return weeks, months, or even years later to within feet of the flush. A beeper collar pinpoints the dog's location on point, although it makes the dog sound like a dump truck backing up, the piercing sound ripping through the deep quiet of the woods. An electronic shock collar extends the hand of discipline, a long leash that in many cases will shock a dog into submission. Unfortunately, the e-collar has ruined countless dogs, and its cruelty when used by the wrong handler is indescribable.

Fortunately, grouse and woodcock hunting remains a relatively simple sport, requiring little specialized gear. What worked a century ago remains valid and effective today. The shotgun has changed little in a century, although we now have interchangeable chokes and more effective shotgun shells thanks to Nobel's smokeless powder, and titanium and aluminum receivers make a modern shotgun up to two pounds lighter. But a grouse hunter can still shoot the same gun a grandfather or great-grandfather shot in the woods decades ago and enjoy the sport as much as a hunter with the most expensive English or Spanish side-by-side. The skill necessary to hit a grouse or woodcock fleeing through the woods remains the same.

For grouse hunters using dogs, a bell and whistle are necessary, but both can be had for less than ten dollars, and they will last for years. Good boots are a requirement, and every hunter needs a pair that fits and feels comfortable. After all, grouse hunting is for the most part a lot of walking, and I tell nonhunting friends that it's mainly a silent sport, punctuated now and then by a shotgun blast. A game bag or a vest, brush pants or chaps, and a blaze orange hat round out the wardrobe.

That grouse hunting remains a relatively straightforward pursuit is one of the reasons why its practitioners find it so appealing. The sport hinges on a simple equation: the cover, the bird, the hunter with a shotgun, and the dog. Modern technology offers grouse hunters few advantages that shortcut experience, fitness, and insight. Skill and fitness matter much more in the pursuit of grouse and woodcock. And best of all . . . both are priceless.

Cover(t)

SOME YEARS BACK I WROTE A PIECE about New Wood, an area of Lincoln County that's one of my favorite places to hunt. The piece was published in an upland hunting magazine, and the next issue carried a letter to the editor from an Illinois bird hunter who wanted to cancel his subscription because my article had "ruined things for him." He claimed that since I'd written about New Wood, "a place he discovered," now everyone would hunt up there and he had to start all over again and find a new place to hunt. An out-of-state hunter, he acted as though he owned the place, as if he had a life lease on the thousands of public acres in New Wood. His reaction wasn't all that uncommon among grouse hunters since we are as jealously territorial as wolves when it comes to guarding our hunting "spots."

Referring to their spots, grouse hunters use *cover* and *covert* interchangeably, as if the *t* made no difference. Cover is the place where animals, people included, can hide, a place offering protection and food, which in the case of grouse means the tangled brush hunters must contend with, the thickets that rip off hats and bloody dogs. It's the flora every grouse hunter must learn to read: those patterns of brook and tag alder, the edge covers where popple meets red oak, the thorn apples way back by the river just past the marsh grass and aspen aged to perfection.

Some experienced hunters can read cover instinctively, knowing just what patterns will or won't hold birds, reading it like a book or a map, understanding it intuitively. The subconscious might play a role, measuring and evaluating cover in ways hunters aren't cognizant of so they can say with some assurance, "That looks birdy," even though they might not be able to explain why it looks that way. It's woodland epistemology.

Covert, however, means "marked by concealment, hidden, secretive." To the grouse hunter a covert conceals birds, and if it happens to conceal a lot of birds, hunters get covert, a sometimes difficult task in a state where most of the grouse and woodcock hunting takes place on public ground. We get abnormally possessive about our coverts—we name them, we start calling them ours, and then we get mad when someone else hunts there. In our minds we "own" them. During the gun deer season, when hundreds of thousands of hunters take to the woods and fields of Wisconsin, these turf wars occasionally turn violent. So far I have yet to hear of grouse hunters physically fighting over hunting grounds, but a scuffle over a spot wouldn't surprise me if it did occur.

Locals, including me, grumble about all the out-of-staters "shooting out" all the good cover. A friend and I once drove over an hour to what he described as a "honey hole," leaving well before sunrise to reach it before anyone else did. (I was surprised he offered to take me there without blindfolding me or swearing I would never hunt there again, which means it wasn't one of his best spots.) We talked about the place as we drove north, so by the time we got there we were jacked up, ready for the hordes of birds that would flush in great clouds before our dogs and guns. I patted the pockets of my vest to reassure myself that I had enough shells for the day. We bumped down the last two-track to the promised land, and then the unthinkable happened: a white truck with Kentucky plates, Ruffed Grouse Society sticker on the topper, sat parked at the gates guarding the entrance to our Eden. Dumbfounded, we gazed and said nothing for several moments. "Bummer," I said finally, and we backed up and drove out, thinking our day ruined.

The day was far from a complete bust, though. We got out the map, drove around the Chequamegon National Forest a bit, found a nice-looking creek, let the dogs out, and worked up it for several hours. We shot some birds and had a wonderful day. And no, don't ask for the name of the road or the creek.

Susan accuses me of keeping all the best coverts for myself. I'll come home some October evening with a couple of birds, the dog tired as only a bird dog can get, and she'll ask, "Where did you go, honey?" I'll answer, and she'll say, "Right. The last time we were there, we hardly put up a bird. No, really, where did you go?" I repeat my answer. She shakes her head and goes back to whatever she was doing before I got home, not believing a word of it. Then a few days later we'll go to someplace new, a place that's looked promising to me for a while. We might see a dozen birds, and on the way home she'll say, "Why haven't you taken me there before? You've been keeping that place to yourself."

"I've never been there before today."

"Yeah, right," she'll say and look at me with that "I didn't just fall off the turnip truck" look.

"I swear. This was the first time." She doesn't believe me.

Susan works as a surgical nurse alongside many surgeons who also hunt grouse. They know we hunt, so during an appendectomy or a hernia repair one might casually ask where we've been hunting lately, hoping she might slip up and blurt out a location. "So you and Mark been out hunting?"

"Sure."

"See many birds?"

"A few."

"Where did you go?"

"Langlade County."

"Ackley?"

"Sure." The Ackley area is over twenty thousand acres large.

"Which side of the road?"

"I can't remember. I'm no good with directions." And so the cat and mouse game goes on all through the appendectomy or the hip replacement.

Once when my brother was up to hunt, I accidentally left my map in his car, and he inadvertently drove back with it to Iowa. This map had all my favorite coverts marked in red ink, along with promising cuttings I check every few years to see how they're coming along. He called a few days later to say he had my map. "I can send it up with a guy from the office," he said. "He's coming up there to grouse hunt." He laughed, but it was no joking matter.

I made him promise that he would mail it to me the next day. I didn't want it in anyone else's hands—it was bad enough that my brother had it.

Gun Lust

STANDING AT AN EXHIBITION CASE at a sporting goods store, I admired the doubleguns inside the glass case— Beretta, Perazzi, Parker, AyA, and Merkel. The dark swirls in the walnut stocks, the hand-tooled designs of quail and grouse and pointing dogs engraved on the receivers, the fine lines and details— all were works of art, meant more for a wall in a walnut-paneled office than for the field. A Merkel 20-gauge side-by-side particularly interested me since my wife's maiden name happens to be the same, and I'm always trying to convince her to buy one. She, however, is perfectly content with her battered Spanish side-by-side.

As I was standing there, two guys came up and looked at the guns briefly and dismissively. One said to the other: "Holy smokes, some of these cost more than my ATV. Who would buy one of these?" They walked away, and I said, "Me." They had no problem spending $5,000 on an ATV but scoffed at the idea of a shotgun costing that much. Me, I'd spend a hundred bucks on a pair of boots and the other $4,900 on a shotgun. I stood there a while longer, then walked away, the thought of breaking the glass and pinching one of the shot-guns crossing my mind.

Like many small-town midwestern boys in the 1960s and '70s, I grew up surrounded by and fascinated with guns in what was clearly a gun culture. My first gun was a Daisy BB gun, a Christmas present when I was ten or so, along with a milk carton of a thousand BBs. I felt rich beyond all measure with a thousand shots.

We played with guns, and today when I hear someone my age bashing violent video games I'm reminded that as kids we often had the real thing in our hands and that the situation on occasion could turn deadly. When I was in grade school, my friend Kerry acciden-tally shot my friend Tom with a .32 caliber breechloader, an old rusted hunk of wood and metal thought to have played a part in the Civil War. The breech wouldn't open and the trigger was rusted solid. We played with that old rusted gun for years, and then one day it went off, the bullet tearing a ragged hole through Tom's hand and lodging in his intestine. I was a block away, having just left Kerry's house, and heard the shot. Tom survived the gunshot, and although it shook us all up, this shooting didn't dampen my relationship with guns.

After my BB gun, my next gun was a Mossberg bolt action .410 with a Monte Carlo stock, a hand-me-down from my father. To make matters worse, it was right-handed and I was left-handed. For a lefty like me, it might simply have been the world's worst pheasant gun, and I never did hit anything flying with that gun.

The first bird I shot flying, a rooster that made the mistake of flushing back toward me in an Iowa cornfield, I brought down with a Stevens singleshot 12-gauge, my first adult gun. I bought that gun for ten dollars from a friend, refinishing the wood and reblueing the barrel and receiver in a high school shop class. In today's climate of weekly school shootings, refinishing a 12-gauge in a high school shop class astonishes me and says something about how our country has changed in the last thirty years.

With that gun I hunted my first ruffed grouse—Iowa birds— with a friend in Winneshiek and Allamakee counties. That gun also brought down my first Wisconsin grouse in Lincoln County when I was in my twenties. But that gun clearly had limitations: a thirty-inch barrel, modified choke, and just one shot. It also had no safety, and the hammer had to be pulled back before each shot and released back into the breech if cocked and not shot. It had a couple of redeeming qualities: it was light in weight, somewhere just under six pounds, and when I got tired of carrying it and grouse were scarce, it would fit broken down in three pieces in my game bag. On the other hand, with the hi-brass loads we shot back in those days, that gun kicked me in the cheek with every shot, although I was too young and hardheaded to notice. Lots of kick was a good thing, I thought, because it meant the gun hit hard.

My future in-laws felt bad for me when they saw my singleshot and lent me a Remington 870 pump for pheasant hunting. It was right-handed, unfortunately, which meant I had to carry the gun at an awkward and unsafe angle, so my left thumb could work the safety. I used that gun several times, but by then I knew what I wanted when I could afford one—a doublegun. Pumps and semiautomatics, shotguns with tube magazines holding at least five shells, never really interested me. This type of gun seemed more suited to the military, and hunting doesn't seem to have all that much in common with war. Besides, nearly all of these guns were made for righties—they had right-handed safeties and ejected spent shells across the face of a left-hander.

When I'd saved enough money, I traded my Stevens singleshot in on my first real shotgun, a Savage 330, a 12-gauge over-and-under made in Finland by Valmet. By the wear and tear visible on it, this gun had shot thousands of rounds, but it was all I could afford at the time. I shot a lot of grouse and woodcock with that gun over the years, especially after having a good gunsmith ream out the top barrel choked full to cylinder. Before that the gun's twenty-six-inch barrels were choked improved modified and full, which threw tight patterns for long shots, clearly making the gun more suited for waterfowling than upland hunting. The gunsmith opened up the pattern for the fifteen- to twenty-yard shots commonly taken on grouse. It shot loose, the hinge pins worn because it had been fired so often, but we had several good years together. My brother, who mainly hunts pheasants in Iowa where he lives, still shoots that old Finnish gun.

That gun felt good in my hands, balanced, and it swung smoothly. On the other hand, it was heavy, and after an all-day hunt I wished for a lighter gun. I had gun lust. I still have gun lust, and, like a drug or alcohol problem, it never seems to go away, simmering away, as it does, under the surface. This is not a condition I admit to many of my friends and colleagues lest they think I'm some sort of gun nut who carries around a truck full of Uzis or someone who sleeps with a loaded handgun in the nightstand. Many of these people would like to see more stringent gun laws, perhaps even the elimination of guns altogether someday. They have never shot a gun, never held a gun in their hands; they're afraid of guns. Usually I don't even mention guns around such a crowd because they might not understand, or worse, not care to understand.

Like any finely wrought tool, though, I find a well-made gun irresistible. As well as beautiful, they're a joy to carry and shoot. Currently I shoot a Browning Superlight Feather 12-gauge, a birthday present from my wife. This is not a best gun—it's mass produced in Japan. Thousands of shotguns are made each year of higher quality, those made in England, Italy, Germany, and Spain, handmade guns costing more than a car with some worth as much as my house. I can't afford such a gun, and if I could afford one I wouldn't feel right carrying it in the woods, where it could get wet, dirty, scratched, and dented. At less than two thousand dollars, I don't feel guilty falling on my Superlight or hunting with it in the rain or snow. Susan wanted to get me something I could have and use for the rest of my life, not a museum piece.

The gun weighs six pounds, four ounces, the second-lightest Citori in the 2000 Browning catalog, so it's about as light as a 12-gauge can get. I love the gun's lines, particularly the English straight stock, which mounts quickly and feels good in my hands, like my favorite hammer or my Swedish ax. Often I pull it out and swing it on imaginary targets around the house, dry firing, like a baseball or golf player would swing a bat or a club in the living room.

Most important, I can hit birds with my Superlight. A hundred-thousand-dollar gun is no good if you can't hit anything with it; a three-hundred-dollar gun is a treasure if it swings right and true. Use what works, any shooting instructor will advise. A friend I occasionally hunt with shoots a side-by-side, and he never tires of kidding me about my over-and-under. "If God intended you to shoot an over-and-under, he would have stacked your eyes one on top of the other," he says. I don't have an answer other than that I've tried to shoot a side-by-side and they just don't feel right. Then again, one of my eyes does seem a bit higher than the other when I look into the mirror. Maybe my friend is right.

Shooting Flying

U P UNTIL THAT POINT, EVERYTHING WORKED with well-oiled precision. The dog had corralled the bird, pinning it under a solitary balsam fir, a nice Christmas tree actually, in the midst of a few widely spaced mature aspens. He had flashed three points working the bird, then coiled into a solid point and didn't show any signs of moving on. By the intensity of his point, it looked as though he had nailed the bird. I moved by the dog on his left side, hoping to flush the bird to my right, a better shot for a left-hander. When I'd eased a few steps beyond the dog, the bird roared off in the general direction expected. Pivoting slightly to my right, I swung the shotgun through the charging bird and pulled the trigger when the barrels had passed through the grouse.

When the wood chips flew, I knew I had missed. My shot slammed into an aspen five yards away, boring a three-inch-diameter hole into the wood, the pattern hardly opening. Concentrating on the bird, I never saw the tree, just the bird, and by the time the miss registered on my brain it was too late to fire the bottom barrel for the bird was gone in a screen of trees and brush. This is a common occurrence as every season I shoot a considerable number of trees.

There was really nothing I could have done to prevent the miss short of side stepping the tree, but then I never accounted for the tree in the first place, so that wasn't going to happen. One of the grouse-hunting books in my library suggests that the astute gunner simply sidestep around such trees in such a situation, as if I were hunting on the carpet in my living room or on the concrete pad of the local trap club. Sticks, brush, other trees, granite stone, and uneven terrain render such a graceful move all but impossible even if I could remember to execute it in the flurry of a flush.

According to George Bird Evans in *The Upland Shooting Life*, we can only expect perfect scores at the trap club, not on wild birds. In the field our shortcomings emerge, particularly when hunting grouse and woodcock in deep woods, which presents additional and often insurmountable challenges. Evans went on to say that "nothing can destroy a man's ego more than trying to shoot grouse," and while I can think of several things more trying to my ego, grouse and an occasional woodcock will sooner, more so than later, humble the most seasoned and accurate shooter.

Evans felt that a good average on grouse was 40 percent of all shots fired. Grouse hunters who never miss are fictional, windbags down at the local bar, or people who shoot stationary birds on the ground or in trees, a shot even a rookie should hit every time. Several factors make grouse difficult birds to hit: habitat, footing, fatigue, and the bird's flight patterns. Woodcock are nearly as difficult, but

since they lie well for the dog, the gunner can get much closer, often nearly stepping on the bird to get it to flush, and then the woodcock flies relatively predictably compared to a grouse. I have yet to see a woodcock dive out of a tree, fly straight for my head, or just mash its way through brush. Even so, their flights are never predictable, flushing as they do in dense woods not in the open.

Grouse tend to be unpredictable when flushed, squirting out from behind or off to the side of a point. Even when pointed, grouse hunters rarely know when and where the bird will come up, and so I stalk a wide circle around the dog pointing, hoping to pin it between me and the dog, but even then I must guess in which direction the bird will fly. Two people are more effective, each taking a side of the point and walking by the dog. Since Susan is right-handed and I'm left, we silently fall into our routine of me coming up on the right and her flushing from the left. Theoretically, a right-hander shoots right-to-left crossing shots better; a left-hander shoots left-to-right crossing shots more effectively. We play the odds.

When grouse do come up, they do so in a flurry of sound and wings, a sound unnerving even after hearing it hundreds of times. Before shooting we must recover, calm ourselves, and then pull the trigger. When the abrupt flush of a grouse, the lightning flash of that moment, ceases to thrill me, it will be time to quit hunting and take up some other pursuit.

Hunters often trek far into the woods pursuing grouse and woodcock. Years ago I roughly calculated I hiked about two miles for every bird in my bag—that's two miles in rough country, not down a concrete sidewalk in the city. According to my pedometer, a gift from my employer during a health initiative, on some hunts I slogged nearly ten miles through tag alder thickets, slash, tamarack bogs, and up and over upland ridges. Going cross-country in the woods is rarely easy. A hunter, even the best conditioned one, will sooner or later tire on such a march, and this fatigue factors into our shooting. It's not like the local trap club, where the trap range is just yards from the parking lot and your gun might weigh as much as eight pounds, whereas my field gun weighs a little over six pounds. The two pounds make a big difference at the end of a long day.

Poor footing accounts for many grouse and woodcock misses, not that missing is such a terrible thing. Fewer game birds, particularly woodcock, would haunt the uplands if we bagged every one we flushed. Missing is practicing conservation, I tell my hunting partners and myself, especially after a long string of misses. If I had a shotgun shell for every time a grouse flushed when my leg was swung over a downed log or I was jumping from tag alder root to tag alder root or my foot was sliding off a damp stone, then I wouldn't need to buy shells for at least one season. A game bird's timing is never that of the hunter.

On the trap or skeet range shooters can afford several seconds to get themselves into a comfortable shooting position. Many develop a routine, what looks like quirks or idiosyncrasies to the rest of us waiting impatiently on the line to shoot. "Get on with it already," we mutter under our breath. Getting comfortable, set, and ready is a luxury in the field, the bird dictating when we shoot, not our command of "PULL!" More often than not, my feet are tangled in briars, tripped up by tree roots, or fumbling over stones, negating whatever smooth swing developed on the shooting range.

Grouse and woodcock haunt the thickest cover imaginable to hide from and evade their multiple predators, including humans. At times their cover is inconceivably thick, particularly to the uninitiated. "We're going to shoot through all that?" my brother asked, pointing at the surrounding brush. An Iowa pheasant hunter, it was his first time in the Wisconsin grouse woods. In the end, a lot of trees die, wood being very effective at stopping lead shot. It's extremely difficult, if not impossible, to account and calculate for all the obstacles a hunter must shoot through at a bird flushing at an obscure angle in heavy cover. Less often, but still very common, a hunter swings through a bird only to have the barrel of the gun whack into a tree or get tangled in brush. This is one reason most effective grouse guns are short, with barrel lengths in the twenty-five- to twenty-six-inch range. A doublegun, which lacks a receiver, will save another four inches over a pump or automatic. A long gun is a slow gun that's more apt to catch on brush, better used in a duck blind or a South Dakota cornfield.

The cover not only shields birds, but it also dictates their erratic flight. Woodcock flush in more consistent patterns than grouse, typically flying up into the treetops, often under dense leaves, before leveling out in the clear to make their escape. Their speed and trajectories, however, are deceptive—they can float butterfly-like, juke and jive like bats after insects, or rocket away quail-like. Overall, though, they tend to flush into whatever opening is presented.

Grouse bull their way through the woods, avoiding only the largest of trunks and limbs. They literally crash through the woods, heedless of whatever is upstream in their way, snapping off twigs and branches in desperate flight. They will also swerve, dive, or climb around obstacles, often at the most opportune moment for them and the most inopportune for the hunter, ruddering hard left or right with their fan-shaped tails just as a hunter pulls the trigger. Once I was swinging on a bird that collided with a branch, stunned itself, and dropped to the ground. It came to after a few moments and wobbled away on its legs, too stunned to fly. It staggered away like a drunk into the woods, hopefully to live another day.

When hunting grouse and woodcock, skill and woodcraft count more than straight runs of a hundred at the trap club, although practice there can only help. Knowing where the birds are helps tremendously, which is why a pointing dog is such a help, giving us a few seconds to get ready to shoot. William Harnden Foster wrote in *New England Grouse Shooting* of the grouse hunter "in the right place at the right time who does the best day in and day out." A little serendipity never hurts, for at the end of the day all the birds are gifts. It never ceases to astound me when one falls at the report of my shotgun. Holding one in hand, I think, *"What have I done to deserve this?"*

The Ruffed Grouse Capital
of the World

D RIVING THROUGH PARK FALLS, WISCONSIN, on Highway 13, a motorist can't help but notice the big round sign
proclaiming the town of about two thousand the Ruffed
Grouse Capital of the World. It's right off the highway next to the
police headquarters and Chamber of Commerce building, big as a
sugar maple, the sign depicting a healthy bird flushing and offering a
nice shot to passersby. Down the road a bit, hunters used to be able
to get a Friday fish fry at the now closed Ruffed Grouse Inn (re-
opened as Alice's), and several other local businesses use the game
bird to promote their trade.

For years I mistakenly thought the Ruffed Grouse Society was
headquartered in Park Falls—the reason for the sign. But that isn't
the case. Park Falls acquired this title in 1985, the Chamber of Commerce having had the wisdom to apply to the state for this trademark,
hence the name, the sign, and its reputation. Such boosterism is

common in northern Wisconsin, whose economy relies heavily on tourism. Just north a dozen or so miles up Highway 13 lies the even smaller town of Glidden, the self-proclaimed black bear capital of the world. On November 23, 1963, a hunter shot a black bear during gun deer season that weighed 665 pounds dressed, a former world record still displayed in a glass case in downtown Glidden at the crossroads of Main Street and County Highway N. Off to the northeast lie Mercer and Hurley, the self-proclaimed loon and snowmobile capitals of the world. To the northwest Hayward bills itself as the muskellunge capital of the world based on the 70-pound behemoth caught east of town on Lake Chippewa in 1949 or the hundred-foot man-made muskie at the Fishing Hall of Fame in town.

No matter how Park Falls claimed its title, the truth is there are a lot of birds around, and one could feasibly make the case for it being the ruffed grouse capital of the world if sheer numbers of birds alone earned the title. The problem, however, is that such a distinction is nearly impossible to measure, as well as equally tough to prove. Grand Rapids, Minnesota, home of the Ruffed Grouse Society's Annual Hunt, would surely contest the title, as would locales and hunters in Maine, the Upper Peninsula of Michigan, and perhaps Ontario or Quebec. Ask grouse hunters from any good area, and they'll probably say hunters don't see more birds anywhere else in the world, the local bias hard to overcome. Well, not all hunters will tell you that. An old veteran, with a wink and a nod, might say he's seen precious few partridge all season, grouse hunters being secretive about their coverts, guarding them jealously and even given to lying on occasion.

Local guide Terry Ides, who with his vizslas has been leading grouse and woodcock hunters around the Park Falls area for over thirty years, says that great numbers of birds, but more importantly accessibility, give the area its reputation. "Our drumming counts are right at the top, but those birds are real easy to get to," said Ides, who has also guided in the Grand Rapids area. The many hunter walking trails, double-tracks, and logging roads help the hunters get at the birds in territory with some of the highest drumming counts in the country.

Ides, who keeps meticulous records of all of his guided hunts, said in 1998 that his average two-person hunt flushed thirty-seven birds per day. These hunters also shot on average forty-four shells per day while bagging 1.3 birds. The numbers are extraordinary, both the high number of birds and the high number of misses. In the late 1990s, at the peak of the cycle, Ides claimed that one of his hunting parties flushed ninety-nine birds in one day, but that didn't come close to the 138 flushed by a party one day in the late 1970s, another peak. As bird numbers cycled upward in the latter part of the first decade of the twenty-first century, hunters around Park Falls once again flushed plenty of birds.

Other local hunters concur with Ides's numbers. A friend of mine who routinely hunts the area with a brace of setters paged through his journals and cited flushing rates similar to Ides's guided trips. He qualified the high numbers, however, since many birds he flushed he only heard or were screened by trees and brush. The trees some years hold onto their leaves until early to mid-October. Birds also covey up in the season's first few weeks, padding those numbers, and some birds might have been flushed more than once (a reflush), inflating the numbers.

According to DNR research biologist Larry Gregg, based in Park Falls, 1998 and 1999 were clearly peak years in the cycle. Drumming counts in northern Wisconsin compared similarly with those of north-central Minnesota, traditionally that state's best grouse region. Gregg said northern Wisconsin averaged 2.0 birds per stop, while Minnesota averaged 2.1, although counts were down 22 percent there. "We're never going to have the aspen acreage that Minnesota has," said Gregg, but he felt flush rates in Park Falls would be similar to those in good habitat in Minnesota and Michigan. The Ruffed Grouse Capital of the World, he added, "isn't something Park Falls wouldn't qualify for."

"We have more ruffed grouse hunters because of the marketing. We certainly have more out-of-state hunters," said Gregg. Some local hunters chafe at the idea of Park Falls as the grouse capital, especially after finding a truck parked at their favorite covert or a half dozen spent casings in their ace in the hole. According to Gregg, however, this double-edged sword does help the local economy and continues the tradition of grouse hunting.

As I write this in the summer of 2009, it looks as though the peak will be delayed a year or two from the ten-year cycle, and Dan Dessecker, director of conservation policy for the Ruffed Grouse Society, felt the peak would be in 2009 or 2010. Fred Strand, the Wisconsin DNR's wildlife manager in Superior, expected the population to peak again in 2010 or 2011, the wet spring of 2008 holding back the peak of the cycle, which bottomed out in 2005.

Only a fool would say Park Falls doesn't have prime upland habitat. Sitting smack in the middle of over a million acres of public forest, it's isolated even by northern Wisconsin standards. The closest sizable towns are Ashland an hour to the north and Wausau about two hours to the southeast. City dwellers could think Park Falls lies in the middle of nowhere, but grouse hunters think it is situated in the middle of everything. Directly east sits a large chunk of the Chequamegon-Nicolet National Forest, and to the south lies the slightly smaller Medford District of the Chequamegon-Nicolet. To the north is the Glidden Ranger District of the Chequamegon. All totaled, grouse hunters have roughly 850,000 acres of national forest in which to hunt.

Just west of Park Falls, the Flambeau River State Forest (90,000 acres), named for the river that runs through its midst, as well as another fork just south of Park Falls, adds thousands more acres to the mix. And finally thousands of acres of Price County Forest and forest crop land (FCL) surround the town of Park Falls. The counties in northern Wisconsin tend to log aggressively, more so than in the state and national forests. And the FCL, privately owned paper company land open to hunting, is logged continuously and aggressively, so hunters can always find the young aspen cuttings that consistently hold birds year after year, although in recent years some of the large holding companies have begun to spin off their land to private individuals who then close it to hunting. Combining all public land— national, state, county, and forest crop—over 1.3 million acres await grouse and woodcock hunters. Like the proverbial kid in a candy store, hunters visiting the area may have too many choices, although most grouse hunters, particularly those from the Northeast and Appalachia, would relish such a problem.

We own a cabin about an hour northwest of Park Falls and frequently drive through it on our way up. In October the Park Falls area is a grouse-hunting mecca—large pickups and SUVs, often pulling aluminum dog trailers, sit parked at restaurants and motels. These late-model vehicles bear plates from Ohio, Pennsylvania, Kentucky, Tennessee, California, and of course Minnesota and Illinois. Even in the down years of the cycle, when there may only be a quarter or a third of the number of birds around as during a peak year, out-of-state vehicles still flash up and down Park Falls, obvious next to the battered and rusted vehicles of the locals.

After coming out of a convenience store in the Ruffed Grouse Capital, I discovered a guy from New York was petting my English setter, who had poked his head out of the rear window of our car. He was outfitted in brand new brush pants, new boots, and a blaze orange Filson packer hat. While petting the dog, he spied the Ruffed Grouse Society sticker on the car's back window. "You a grouse hunter?" he asked.

I said, "Occasionally."

"You ever hunt around here?"

"Sometimes."

"We only put up two birds all day—six hours and only two damn birds. I didn't even get off a shot. Being a local and all, you must have some good spots, eh?"

The lie slipped out instinctively. "Me? I haven't seen hardly a partridge all year."

Nine Mile Stump

THERE'S A PLACE IN A SECTION of the Marathon County forest where a graveyard of blackened stumps rises volcanically out of the soil: ancient, massive, charred, and rotting. These stumps in the Nine Mile section are all that's left of the virgin white pine that just 150 years ago towered above northern Wisconsin, so I come here and pay respect to what once was. I pull on rubber boots to get back to the stumps because they're beyond a tag alder swamp and across a creek, a humid blackfly- and mosquito-infested place in summer.

One stump in particular stands out in this bottomland, and at least once a year I hike back in to see how it's weathered the year. I try to go during the woodcock flight, for on the way there and back I may see a bird or two or perhaps a grouse. I hope for a point from the dog, a fleeting shot, and just maybe a bundle of feathers in my game bag.

Ironically, in the white pine days before the first big cutting, few, if any, grouse or woodcock would have lived here because they don't do well in virgin timber; they thrive in second-growth aspen, and continued clear-cutting ensures that popple will flourish in this corner of the county forest. On the other hand, looking at the stumps I sense a great loss and can't help but wonder what it would have felt like to stand among these great trees.

While among these stumps, I sometimes dream of that virgin forest, the sights, smells, and sounds in those old woods. And what did the men who crosscut these stately trees think as they sawed through three or four feet of living wood and a two-hundred-foot white pine crashed to the forest floor with a resounding thump, a noise felt more through the soles of the boots than heard, taking with it several smaller trees, bouncing back up again, and finally settling back to earth, limbs aquiver, leaving a gaping hole in the sky. What crossed their minds? Power? Progress? Pay? The thought of several thousand board feet of lumber created with one back-wrenching cut? Maybe they were amazed, cutting upward of half a million board feet on an average forty-acre tract. Who knows what each thought while lugging a heavy saw at the end of a short winter day, looking back over their shoulders at a field of fresh, yellow stumps weeping sap, the signature of their labor? Most likely they were just doing their job.

Who can blame these hardworking Swedes, Finns, and Norwegians, men who knew wood and felt at home in the north woods? Certainly not me since I enjoy building with wood, my cabin frame employing several massive posts and beams. Besides, these men were only trying to survive in the so-called New World, a place they may have thought their labor would build and improve.

My favorite stump in this Nine Mile cutting is over forty-three inches in diameter—I measured it once with a tape—and is molding quietly in a small clearing. It's as though the live trees have respectfully given the old stump some room. Who knows how tall the tree once stood above the nearby marsh? The middle has rotted away; only the ragged and moldy sides of the stump remain. These remains one day will collapse and fold back into the rich, moist soil, feeding other trees to come. The blackened skeleton reveals the foundation of a giant, however. Forest fires ravaged northern Wisconsin in the 1930s and burned these stumps, preserving them in a charcoal-like state.

While backcountry skiing, I first came across the forty-three-inch stump, easily picking up the black against the surrounding fresh white snow. Feeling as though I'd stumbled across an obscure grave marker, I looked up into the winter sky and tried to imagine the height of this once majestic tree, how it would look compared to the second-growth popple thriving there now.

These stumps punctuate the north woods—they're there if we have the eyes to see their unassuming forms. The stumps, almost exclusively white pine, stand out best when the leaves are off the trees and a bit of snow covers the ground, just a hint of snow, not enough to bury their subtle forms. In ideal stumping conditions, sometime in November, it's easy to pick out the charred wood against the subdued browns and grays of autumn, but the stumps also stand out in early spring just as the first greens of April spring forth from the awakening earth, around bloodroot and dogtooth violet time, just as the woodcock begin their sky dance. Once in early April after a late spring snowstorm, I nearly skied over on a partially frozen woodcock back in there, looking woefully out of place in the winter weather.

After coming across these stumps the first time, I asked a friend—a forester who knows and respects trees, a founder of the Big

Tree Society—about these stumps, and he said they were all that was left of the virgin timber in Marathon County. He thought he knew the very stump, saying it was charred because much of northern Wisconsin went up in flames in the dry years of the Depression when the slash left after logging ignited like kindling and created raging fires. The tree, he guessed, was probably felled around the turn of the century. He also said the first cutting is the best thing for grouse and woodcock, and that he'd heard stories from old hunters about the hunting when the second growth flourished. One old hunter he knew drove to town as a kid with his dad, a ten-mile trip in a horse-drawn wagon, plunking away with his .22 at the then unwary birds. He'd fill a barrel, sell them in town for a dime apiece, and the family would purchase flour and sugar with the proceeds. Today Wisconsin game laws forbid trafficking in both grouse and woodcock.

After discovering my first stump, I started to see others—while hiking, mountain biking, cross-country skiing, even while driving down the highway. But mostly I saw them while hunting, bush-whacking slowly and deliberately in places I would never travel in other seasons. Before happening across the Nine Mile stump, I couldn't see the stumps for the forest, stumps there for well over a century. Like good grouse or woodcock habitat, the stumps are there if one will only look, reminders of all we miss as we scurry through life.

Knowing Our Limits

WE DON'T LIKE TO SPEAK AND THINK of limits, of pre-scribing and curtailing our behavior. Americans like things bigger, better, and faster. We don't like to be told how fast to drive. We don't want to cut back on the size of our homes, the calories we eat, or the hours of TV we watch. Although we often try to limit our number of drinks, we often don't succeed in sticking to that number. And many Americans are spending more money than we make, exceeding our limits, not only those self-imposed but also those from banks and credit card companies. *Limit* is a four-letter word in our limitless culture.

In the sporting world, however, the word *limit* has a different meaning. Getting a limit (the prescribed number of game birds or fish the state dictates one can legally take) is the definition of a suc-cessful day in the field or on the water, and so the limit becomes the goal. If the limit of walleyes on a particular lake is four, then that's what a fisher will angle for. If it were forty, then that would be the new target, even if such a mark were impossible to reach. It's an un-intentional carrot the DNR dangles in front of hunters and anglers.

In my wife's pheasant-hunting family in Iowa, it's a tradition to dance the limit jig, which in Iowa means three roosters. My brother-in-law Steve executes a combination hornpipe and Russian jig in his heavy clodhoppers, something he picked up in Russia from his in-laws we suspect. He also tells the story of almost limiting on the way to his mailbox at the old Iowa farmhouse he used to rent along the Nishnabotna River in southwestern Iowa. He shot two birds and missed a third while walking his long driveway to and from his mailbox. My nephew Evan's limit jig looks like he's listened to too much gangster rap, and his dad Wes looks like a white guy dancing, moving his head and fingers. I refuse to do the limit jig, claiming I can't dance, my usual excuse in any dancing situation, but once I was pressed so hard to do something I jumped up in the air and clicked my heels together like a leprechaun, no easy task with three heavy roosters in a game bag. For sure, I looked rather cloddish.

In Wisconsin a hunter can legally shoot five grouse and three woodcock per day, not that doing so happens very often. For instance, during the 2008 season I didn't once take a limit of either grouse or woodcock. In poor years, such as 2004 and 2005, hunters were lucky to see five grouse per day let alone shoot at five. It is much easier to limit on woodcock, particularly when the flight birds are down from Canada on their migration south, the upland hunter's version of manna from heaven. Woodcock hold tightly for the dog, and often they only fly thirty or forty yards to be reflushed if one wishes. On good days my dogs might point fifty woodcock, and several points might yield more than one bird. Four woodcock once flushed from one of Ox's points, which startled me so that I didn't fire. When

I started hunting woodcock two decades ago, the limit was six, but three is more reasonable, especially since woodcock populations have been steadily declining for the last thirty years. In fact, Woodcock Limited, a wildlife group recently formed that understands the precarious nature of the woodcock population, hopes to persuade its members to limit their take of the bird.

When I was younger and obsessed with the grouse limit, the magic number five was the symbol of my success as a hunter. A limit meant accurate shooting, good dog work, and a knowledge of the woods. I thought all successful hunters routinely bagged a limit. It was like shooting par or batting .300, scoring four touchdowns or getting a hat trick. It was a numbers game, a way to compare myself with the rest of the competition.

Some ten Octobers ago a friend and I thought about entering a competitive grouse hunt after seeing a flyer. The first pair of hunters to bag ten birds would win. If no teams bagged ten, then the team with the most would be declared the winner. Wandering into a local bar for a burger and a beer, Ross and I found out about this contest one evening after a long day of hunting. The bar was sponsoring this hunt and had signs posted on telephone poles in the parking lot, on the door, in the bathroom, and taped to the mirror behind the bar. We figured we had good dogs, we were young and fit, let's do it.

On the way home, we discussed the matter. When our enthusiasm had tempered and we were thinking more rationally, we realized any contestant could hunt as he or she deemed fit. A hunter could drive the back roads and shoot sitting birds, a much easier and even more effective technique than hunting grouse with a pointing dog. Or a hunter could shoot birds out of trees. Respecting the quarry and a sense of fair chase would only penalize a hunter, who had nothing to lose in this game. The grouse, however, were playing for mortal stakes. By the time we had driven halfway back to Wausau, we had changed our minds about entering the contest.

Never have I regretted staying away from that grouse shoot. In fact, from that day forward I started to define success in the field in different terms. Keeping track of my score was no longer so important to me, as if one could play against nature. And truthfully if I were keeping accurate score the grouse win 80 to 90 percent of the time regardless of my superior intellect, superior technology, and the help of a good dog. Even when we think we are dominating nature, we aren't.

The numbers matter less partially because I have a better grasp of my own limits. Still I have yet to live by the higher laws Thoreau writes of in *Walden*. He thought all boys should be introduced to hunting and trusted they would outgrow this pursuit as he did, but I have yet to leave my gun behind. Although Thoreau left his fowling piece at home, he was still tempted to fish, admitting that he had a certain instinct for it. "But I see that if I were to live in a wilderness I should again be tempted to become a fisher and a hunter in earnest."

Killing is no longer as important to me as it once was, and the temptation to score my birds and compare myself to other hunters fades with each passing season. Even so, the predatory instinct that Thoreau seemed to despise in himself stirs my blood every fall, and hunting feels natural or instinctual to me come late September. If buying our meat in the supermarket, or worse yet at a fast food joint, is how we remain civilized, then count me among the barbaric and uncivilized.

Getting Lost, Staying Lost

"Are you sure you know where we are?" Charlie asked.

"Yeah."

"You sure? Because I have to be back in town by five." Charlie, who has a faulty and inconsistent sense of direction, wanted reassurance. "You know where we are," he said again. This time it sounded more like a statement than a question.

"The river is to the south, over that hill. If we had to, we could walk it east out to the road. We're fine. Let's hunt toward that spruce or balsam, that green tree." I pointed with my barrel to the only coniferous tree in our direction, a spire-shaped balsam fir.

To be fair to Charlie, we had hiked into some claustrophobia-inducing popple. We could see a scant twenty or thirty yards ahead, and the spruce we were orienting toward was only visible because it towered above the surrounding trees. Grouse and woodcock hunting requires navigating in dense cover, sometimes when the leaves still cling to the trees. Oftentimes the cover lies in lowland, bordering impenetrable swamps and seeps. It's easy to get turned around and confused, and even after a couple of decades spent hunting this type of cover, I still get twinges of claustrophobia. When that happens, I like to walk trails or get on the edge of thick cover instead of in the middle of it. Invariably, though, the dog goes on point, and I find myself right back in the thick of things.

We like to know where we are at all times, whether we're traveling down the highway or wondering how we did on our last test or if we're making any money on our investments. We hate to go astray, and so we have invented technology, most notably GPS, to keep us on the straight and narrow. But as the civilized world grows ever more complex and unfamiliar we find ourselves bewildered even more frequently. We often lose our way in the urban jungle, and yet the woods and wilderness confuse twenty-first-century man even more, which is one of the reasons why so few people feel comfortable in the wild anymore. There are no road signs, no broad and level streets, no people to get directions from, and this confuses and frightens us.

It's quite simple to get lost while grouse hunting. All one has to do is stop paying attention for a few moments. I have been lost just a few times or many times depending on how one defines *lost*. If *lost* means not knowing exactly where I am, I get lost quite a bit, dozens of times per season. Once while hunting with my brother and his co-worker Curt, we got "turned around," as all the cover started to look vaguely unfamiliar. After an hour or so, we spotted a road in the distance and made for it, but when we got to it I realized it wasn't the road I had expected to find. My brother looked at me reading my compass, taking a bearing on a white pine on a far-off ridge, and said, "You don't know where we are, do you?"

"Yes, I do. Close enough."

"He's lost, Curt."

"No, we're not. I know exactly where we're at."

"Where?"

"Right here . . . in Lincoln County."

I trusted the compass, they trusted me—what other choice did they have—and we walked southward until we cut the gravel road, the one I'd originally hoped to find, and we followed it back to the car. While lost we detoured around a couple of broad swamps, crossed a creek, and spent a couple more hours in the woods than we had anticipated, but we did eventually make it back to the car before dark. Although it may seem like Wisconsin has millions of acres of wilderness, a person is never very far from a road. According to a friend, the largest roadless section in the state is only six miles across, but again that all depends on how we define *road*.

And yet all those trees and all that wildness do make us uneasy at times. One time years ago, I lost my compass. It must have fallen out of my pocket after I shot a grouse and kneeled down to gather it from the dog and slide it in my game bag. I got turned around in a young cutting as the sun started to set, and when I reached into the pocket of my vest for my compass it wasn't there. Nor was it in the other pockets or the pockets of my pants. In an instant I panicked; my heart rate hammered in my ears, and my breathing quickened. I upped my pace, and walked one way, then another, until I was running—in circles. Soon Venus was a bright prick of light in the darkening sky, and the stars were coming out. The sun had long set. Realizing the futility of my situation, I finally sat down and leaned against a tree. The dog looked at me as if I were ill. No doubt he knew where we were. He was hungry and wanted to go home. What were we waiting for?

At that moment, I resigned myself to spending the night in the woods. It was October, and the temperature would drop with the clear sky, but it didn't feel like it would go below freezing. We would get cold, but we would survive. Susan would worry herself sick and no doubt call the authorities, which would embarrass me. But as I calmed down leaning against that tree in the darkening woods and stopped listening to the panic in my head, I heard the faint hum of a highway off to the south. I knew it ran dead east-west in a straight line. I got up, and so did the dog, and made off in the direction of the cars whooshing down the highway. It was dark when we cut the highway and darker when we got back to the car. When I got home, Susan scolded me and said she was about ready to dial the police. I had almost made the paper.

In this same section of county forest, one evening a few years later, Susan and I ran into a clearly distraught hunter in the parking lot as we were about to leave. "Did you see another hunter back in there?" he asked us. We had seen no one. "Jim's got a bad heart, too." We couldn't drive off after he said that and walked back down the trail a ways, yelling and hollering with Jim's friend. He fired his shotgun several times. Nothing. The woods were quiet. By then it was dark and the situation serious. Jim's friend asked if we would drive to the bar ten miles down the road, call Jim's son, and tell him to bring an ATV. We left him there at the parking lot in case Jim showed up and needed assistance.

We were naturally concerned as we drove toward the bar, both of us suspecting the worst. When I rang up Jim's son, he sounded upset, almost as if we were bothering him needlessly. After listening to him complain for a bit, I said, "Hey, I'm just giving you the message. He's *your* dad."

We debated whether we should go back to the parking lot because the son had been such a jerk on the phone, but we did. When we got back, the lot was empty. Jim was obviously okay, so we quickly turned around and drove off because we didn't want to run into the son. A few miles down the road, we did meet him coming at us in the other lane of the county highway with the ATV on a trailer. I looked at Susan, laughed, and said, "And I thought he was mad on the phone. Wait until he pulls into an empty parking lot."

This was in the days before cell phone use was widespread. Even so, way out where we were was well beyond cell phone range. Many of the places where I hunt are beyond the long reach of the cell phone, and that's OK with me. A GPS device works anywhere, but I don't carry one because it doesn't seem like appropriate technology to use out in the woods. I'm a bit of a technophobe, afraid of bringing too much of our modern civilization into what's left of Wisconsin's wild country lest it become like the place I hope to leave behind, at least for a while each autumn. Besides, getting lost and staying that way for a while isn't always a negative thing, for I've stumbled across a lot of new country I wouldn't have found had I stayed in my familiar and comfortable ruts. Nowadays, though, I do carry a second compass.

LATE SEASON

Confessions of a Grouse Hunter

THIS IS DIFFICULT FOR ME TO ADMIT, but just about every autumn around the middle of November I grow weary of grouse hunting, struggling through the aspen stands and alder thickets of northern Wisconsin. Maybe it's claustrophobia from the close woods. I try not to admit it, even to myself, but I dream of the days when I pheasant hunted as a boy in Iowa, of a single pheasant flushing into open cobalt skies over a windswept slough down south in Iowa.

To hardcore grouse hunters this may sound heretical, especially coming from a card-carrying member of the Ruffed Grouse Society and the Loyal Order of Dedicated Grouse Hunters. This is blasphemy coming from one who swears by the effectiveness of a pointing dog and a doublegun. After all, any grouse hunter worth his brush pants thinks the ruffed grouse is the king of game birds.

You see, grouse hunters, the serious ones anyway, tend to act elitist, at times downright snobbish. We read the right books—those by George Bird Evans, William Harnden Foster, and Burton Spiller—and somehow we have come to think every other bird plays second fiddle to the ruffed grouse, with the possible exception of its goofy-looking colleague, the woodcock, which resides in close proximity to grouse, so it can't be all that bad. Every now and then we shoot a brace of woodcock to go with our grouse.

Grouse hunters shoot the right guns: small-gauge doubles, not pumps or autoloaders. We cringe at the very thought of a big-bore Remington 870 pump gun. Heavy and improperly balanced, an autoloader is even more ludicrous. Besides, who needs five shells when two, nay one, should be able to handle the job. We wear the right clothes: $250 Gore-Tex boots and waxed canvas double-layer brush pants. We don't hunt in the same clothes we use to change the truck's oil. We use the right dog: a pointer, preferably an English variety, maybe a continental breed but never a flushing dog or retriever. We shoot a crafty, indigenous bird, the prize of the continent, not one brought over from China like the pheasant, one that's made a shooting preserve of the entire Great Plains.

Our idea of perfection is an old, abandoned apple orchard bordered on three sides by stone fences against a backdrop of misty gray mountains. In the foreground an English setter stands rigid, tail straight up, the signal flag. Two grouse have flushed in a clear arena, one right, one left, and still the dog holds. Swinging his side-by-side left then right, the old hunter nails the well-rehearsed double. This picture hangs on my wall.

To be perfectly honest, though, this picture doesn't come close to mirroring my grouse-hunting experiences. I start to hanker after pheasants on days like the one when I scratched my cornea in a thorn apple thicket and thought I would have to crawl out of the woods on hands and knees. It felt like someone had shoved a fork in my eye. I come unhinged after a day when all the birds refuse to hold for the dog and scoot away under balsam firs, away from solid point after solid point.

Then there are the days I spend trudging through blackberry gauntlets and popple cuttings, tripping, falling, and landing on my shotgun, only to hear the birds flush without ever actually seeing one. And finally if and when I do glimpse one clear enough to shoot at, I slam the ends of my barrels against a popple just as I'm about to pull the trigger. I can count my clear shots each autumn on one hand. It's enough to make me want to shoot birds on the ground or up in trees, a mortal sin for the serious grouse hunter.

Then there are the ticks—legions of ticks, wood and deer, carriers of the dreaded Lyme disease and anaplasmosis. Do you ever wonder if God created these creatures to keep us out of the woods? One of my favorite coverts is a tick heaven, and no doubt a Lyme disease hell, but I keep going back there, drawn like a moth to a street lamp, because I always put up a lot of birds. Once, after a run through there, we pulled well over a hundred ticks off our setter.

Fortunately for me, my wife is from southwestern Iowa and comes from a family steeped in pheasant hunting and blessed with plenty of spots in which to hunt. Places like Bogue Ditch and Big Buck Ditch. We traditionally hunt there during the long Thanksgiving weekend, and occasionally I get out in December with my brother, who lives in central Iowa.

Down there my relatives never let me forget that I'm a grouse hunter, though. They needle me about shooting too quickly, which I do because I'm so used to snap shooting in the woods as soon as possible, as soon as I get a literal window of opportunity. They roar with laughter when I whiff on an easy straightaway bird, but then again they are fairly democratic about laughing at anyone who misses an easy shot, and the hard ones as well. Equal opportunity jeering rules the day.

They send me down into the nastiest cover, the razor-wire multiflora rose, because they claim I'm used to the thick stuff. "It'll feel just like up north," they say. "And maybe you'll hit something down there in all that brush." They tell me my setter looks goofy next to the Weimies and shorthairs or that he will get stuck full of cockleburs with all that long hair, which he usually does. They ask why I hang a bell around my dog's neck so he sounds like a cow. They might even wonder if I press my pants before a hunt—though they have yet to ask.

Some years, though, I feel a need to hunt pheasants before Thanksgiving, and one November years ago my pheasant fever got so bad I decided to give Wisconsin birds a try and headed south to public land—a chunk ten thousand acres large managed specifically for pheasants. We walked six hours and put up three birds—all ruffed grouse and all nice shots. I was so keyed on pheasants that I watched all three fly away, thinking they were hen pheasants and therefore not legal birds. By the third flush, you'd think I would have learned my lesson. Disillusioned about Wisconsin pheasant hunting and my game bag empty, I drove home.

I have shot one pheasant in Wisconsin, just one, but this was incidental to a grouse hunt. I was deep in the woods just south of the New Wood area, a well-known Wisconsin grouse and woodcock cover, hunting with Dan, the breeder of my English setter. We were working my dog Ox and his grandfather Black Jack that day and had had good luck, shooting a pair of grouse and several woodcock. At one time we had two dogs simultaneously on point on two different birds. Toward the end of the day, both dogs got birdy along an alder run, classic grouse and woodcock cover. It's incomprehensibly dense stuff, especially to hunters used to western skies. One friend calls tag alders monkey trees, I think because they're so junglelike. You really can imagine monkeys swinging around in these woody arbors.

At any rate this particular bird was running, but the dogs finally pinned it near a clump of balsam fir at the end of the tags. I moved in, and the bird rose up, cackling, big as a zeppelin. It was a rooster, brilliantly colored and looming large. It looked about as out of place in the north woods as a Japanese subcompact in Detroit. I swung on the bird, firing when it was maybe twenty yards out, and it dropped like a stone. I will never forget that rooster, a long-spurred wild bird, or the shot and the pheasant pie we had for supper the next evening. We had no idea what he was doing down in the tag alders in the middle of big woods, so far from any cover he could have called home. There wasn't a farm field within five miles, and the nearest corn, his food source, was even farther away. By the look of his long spurs, that old rooster had survived at least one hard Wisconsin winter: the lack of food, subzero temperatures, and deep snowpack that sometimes lasts four months.

Pheasants, for many reasons, have sunk their spurs into my soul. It's the first upland bird I shot, and they say you never forget the first one. Maybe my passion stems from the cliché that claims you can take the boy out of Iowa but you can't take Iowa out of the boy. Whatever it is, I still count working a November slough meandering through a picked cornfield in hopes of kicking up a rooster as one of life's finer things.

But as a grouse hunter with a reputation to uphold, I don't like to admit this, not even to myself.

Grouse Weather

EVERY ONCE IN A WHILE, I happen across surprising numbers of grouse massed together in just a few brief acres. A
couple of years ago on a cold November Saturday, my
dog went on point in a small grassy depression carved out of the
thousands of acres of surrounding popple and balsam fir. The clearing was less than an acre. It was a cold morning, frost still riming the
long grass, and a weak sun had yet to melt it off. I moved in front of
the dog, and the bird got up and flushed into the clearing, presenting
a relatively easy shot.

We moved four more birds in that small depression, maybe fifty
yards in circumference, all hunkered down in the grass, surprising
them in their warm beds. To the west there were more grassy depressions, little kettles encircled by heavy woods, so we moved on and
hunted them. Sure enough, we found birds in the next little savanna,
all tucked in, holding tight, refusing to leave their snug quarters.
After hunting that second depression, we had enough grouse for the
day, but we pressed on to check more of these grassy openings and

test my hunch that they would hold birds. Grouse flushed from nearly every one, for once presenting relatively easy shots, and when the morning ended, we had moved well over two dozen birds holed up in the grass, protecting themselves from a cold November day.

The following September, on an unseasonably cold morning, I hunted those same depressions again, thinking we would encounter like numbers. This time we didn't move a single grouse. The birds were up in the popples on the ridges or down in the tag alders along the creeks, just about everywhere except where we had surprised them the previous November. And rightly so—it was a somewhat warmer day, and the grouse were out foraging, not hunkered down in thick cover conserving body heat.

Article after article has been written about locating grouse by examining their crops and locating those food sources. And we do find grouse near their food, but weather may affect their habits, and habitations, just as much, maybe more. Slowly over the years, through my experiences and by talking with other hunters, I've come to realize that weather more so than diet plays the crucial role in finding birds.

A few writers have discussed the effects of weather on ruffed grouse, most notably George Bird Evans. He wrote in *The Upland Shooting Life* that weather, more than food or cover, affects grouse shooting. Weather (cold hands, a wet trigger) affects the hunter's competence. Weather influences the location of birds, how they act, and a hunter's chances of locating them. Evans felt weather affected scent, "the most critical factor of dog work." In this classic text Evans devotes ten pages (as many as he writes about diet) to weather and the role it plays in grouse hunting.

In most areas across North America where ruffed grouse live, the weather can change from summerlike on opening weekend to bitterly cold at the season's end—a phenomenon Evans recognized. Where I hunt in north-central Wisconsin, the ambient temperatures can swing well over 100 degrees in the course of the season, from a balmy 80 in mid-September to a brutal minus 25 or lower in January. Sun, wind, rain, heat, drought, sleet, snow, frost—grouse and grouse hunters experience it all.

The warm, windy days of the early season offer perhaps the most difficult hunting conditions of the entire season. The northern woods seem junglelike, home to hordes of mosquitoes and scads of deer and wood ticks, but it's the lush green leaves screening the birds that really affect shooting. Plus in dry years grouse can hear dog and man coming a long way off, the brittle leaves and twigs on the forest floor crunching underfoot. For whatever reason, grouse seem especially skittish on windy days when the leaves are off the trees. Some hunters believe this is because they can't hear the approach of predators. Couple wind with dry leaves, and a grouse hunter might be lucky just to get a fleeting glimpse of a bird on a breezy, dry fall day. Warm and dry air also creates scenting problems for dogs, the scent dissipating more readily in the thinner air, which only compounds the misery of these hot hunts. On calm, wet days, scent hangs in the air, and a misty day between 40 and 50 degrees seems to be the ideal grouse-hunting day.

On windy, dry days when I had two dogs, I hunted my Weimaraner since he hunted closer than my setter, who ranged much farther out, often beyond earshot on windy days. It's easier to hear a close-working dog, to find it on point, and to hear any birds it might bump. If the birds flush wild, which they tend to do in windy conditions, it's still possible, though not likely, to get a shot off with a close-working dog.

In dry conditions we look for birds near water, so we hunt near creeks and tag alder seeps. This also makes sense, since the dog can drink and cool off in the water and we can refill the dog's water bottle. Working older, more open stands also makes sense since longer shots are possible among the widely spaced trees. Evans suggests that we "pass up brush for the cool, tall woods" on hot days when the leaves are still out. Working young popple stands is an exercise in futility, a chance to merely hear birds flush in the distance, as well as an exercise in claustrophobia.

Fortunately, the warmth of September soon gives way to the cold and rain, sleet and snow of late autumn. Gordon Gullion wrote that grouse abhor wet feet, and to keep their feet dry they often fly up into trees and brush. They tend to hold tighter, staying put in thickets until a predator puts them out. Some of my best hunting has come on calm, wet days when the birds are reluctant to leave dry cover. On wet days it's easier to approach grouse. Crunching leaves or snapping twigs don't give predators away, and the birds seem to lie better for the dogs, particularly for pointing breeds. Evans felt that scenting improved on cool, wet days. "Scent," he believed, "like the steam off the dogs' coats, seems to hover about the grouse, held there by damp air."

In heavy downpours grouse favor conifers: spruce and balsam, maybe a pine. In lighter rain and drizzle they might flush out of popple or from the tops of tag alders. On wet days I scan the trees, paying special attention to my dogs, especially when they tilt their muzzles back and reach with them as high as they can, searching for scent riding high in the heavy air. The problem with hunting in wet conditions is that we quickly get soaked not just from the rain coming down but also from all of the moisture collected on grass and leaves. Knocking about under young trees sends shower after shower down on a bird hunter, more moisture than most rain gear can handle, and this kind of weather makes me think about a cup of coffee and the woodstove back home.

Birds in trees make scenting and pointing difficult, and a flushing dog might have an advantage over a pointer in this situation. Still, nothing gives me more satisfaction than a bird pointed in a tree. Grouse feel relatively safe from ground predators while in trees, so they normally stay put, which gives hunters an opportunity to observe their behavior. Perched in trees, grouse like to stretch to their full height, as if they could blend in with the rest of the tree. Usually it takes shaking the tree or throwing a stick to get the bird to flush. Just recently, it took three sticks and finally a direct body hit to get a treed grouse to flush. Unfortunately, it's nearly impossible to shoot after throwing a stick, especially if one is hunting alone and trying to manage both the throwing and the shooting. It doesn't help that a grouse diving out of a tree is the hunter's most difficult shot, the arc of the bird an uncharacteristic flight pattern.

Even in the early season, birds may exhibit the tendency to flush from trees or tag alders. Perhaps this is because of the higher proportion of juvenile birds using trees to avoid ground predators. These young birds seem to feel safe in trees in early season (mid-September to early October in Wisconsin) high up behind the cover of leaves. After the leaves fall, birds in deciduous trees become targets, food for hawks and owls. With the leaves down, grouse spread throughout the woods, no longer confining themselves to popple and tag alder thickets. In winter grouse return to aspen for buds, this being one of their December and January staples in northern Wisconsin. I don't hunt much in winter after the snow flies, but I've been startled dozens of times while cross-country skiing when birds flush out of popples. When this happens, I pray for their success in making it through the long, dark winter, their chances of dying before spring greater than their chances of seeing the woods green up again.

A few inches of snowfall cover their food on the ground and force them to seek food in trees. During our recent gun deer season, which opened in mid-November, I watched several grouse plowing with difficulty through six inches of fresh snow on the ground. Picking buds off trees has to be easier than foraging on the ground, and fit birds soon learn to fly into aspens for a dinner of buds. Fresh snow isn't all bad, though, especially deep powder. Grouse in the northern part of their habitat dig or dive into this insulator, which ironically can be much warmer than the ambient air temperature. In times of brutal cold and little snow cover, grouse congregate in dense cover such as conifers or thick brush, the trees at least breaking the wind. On sunny winter days, or any cold morning for that matter, grouse congregate on warm southern exposures, often places where the snow has melted and even more heat collects, absorbed by the dark earth. A friend said he once surprised over a dozen birds on one such exposure, but he was so stunned he missed with both barrels.

Like people, grouse respond to the weather. Let's face it—on gloomy, gray mornings we have difficulty crawling out of bed. Grouse do, too. Understanding the effects of weather may help us find a bird or two, sometimes still snuggling in bed.

A Fall of Woodcock

A S I WALKED A LOGGING ROAD toward a creek bordering the county forest, the dog quartered in young aspen on my left. After a bit he crossed the road and moved to my right, angling through the skinny trees, his nose to the ground. Behind us a few hundred yards, a car whooshed past on the gravel road. The dog was old, stumbling on occasion over sticks and rocks, so I wanted to keep him near the road in case something happened. It was early November, a cool and cloudy Monday afternoon, the final afternoon of the forty-five-day woodcock season.

Working down the slope toward the creek and the tag alders there, the dog started to slow. His stubby tail wagged ever so slightly, like a slow metronome, but after thirteen seasons following behind him I knew from that wag that he was working game, from the looks of the cover probably a woodcock. When the dog eased into a point and then looked out of the corner of his eye at me, I moved off the logging road and into the popple. I approached the dog and passed him on his left. He reminded me of a sprinter in the blocks before the hundred-meter dash, keyed up and ready to bolt at the sound of the starter's pistol. I circled around the dog, his tail still flagging slowly, and searched the ground a few yards in front of the dog. After a few moments, the dog relaxed and eased out of his point, no longer so sure of the scent. The woodcock had been here, though, with fresh droppings (also called whitewash or chalk) evidence that they had been around as recently as that morning. Even though the season was still on, the last of the woodcock had moved on, driven south by the hard frost, lured to a warmer climate.

The first time I ever kicked up a woodcock was when I was a young Iowa boy pheasant hunting with a family group. We were working a small wooded creek that sliced through a picked cornfield. Dogless, we figured we would push the pheasants down the slough toward the far gravel road, where the roosters would get nervous, flush, and with any luck fall to our guns. Partway down the slough, a small dun-colored bird with a long bill twittered up from under my feet and zigzagged down the draw. It startled me, but from my reading I recognized it as a woodcock, a bird legal to shoot. As a kid I read everything about hunting, even the Iowa game regulations, so I knew about woodcock. The bird flew low and just a few feet above the dead grass. I pulled back the hammer on my singleshot, pulled the trigger, and whiffed, providing everybody with a good laugh. That I would even shoot at such a trite thing amused the group even more than my miss.

Such a prejudice against the diminutive bird wasn't and isn't unusual. A friend told me a story about a hunting partner who one day while hunting grouse shot and left to rot eleven woodcock on his land. "I hate those suckers," he told my friend. He reasoned that since it was his property he could do what he wanted on it, with it, and to it, including the slaughter of woodcock.

Most Wisconsin bird hunters don't shoot woodcock on sight, but they often hold a prejudice against the bird for a variety of reasons. Our prejudice may stem from the comparatively small size of woodcock, the adult males weighing between 125 grams (4½ ounces) and 165 grams (6 ounces) and the adult females between 165 and 220 grams (8 ounces), according to William Sheldon in *The Book of American Woodcock*. In the hierarchy of game birds, its small size places it well below the grouse in most hunters' minds because size often matters. And since the woodcock and grouse seasons run concurrently, most upland gunners spend their days in the woods pursuing the more "noble" ruffed grouse. To them woodcock are an interesting sideshow at best.

Perhaps this thinking is a holdover from the meat-hunting days of our forefathers. For most of our history on this continent, American families supplemented their diets with wild game, and hunting was a matter of calories rather than sport or tradition. Shotgun shells were expensive, often bought by the handful rather than the box, so it's understandable why woodcock were not and still are not prime targets for upland hunters. They are hard to hit and offer little reward, a few ounces of dark meat. A turkey or grouse offered considerably more meat per shot and could often be swatted on the ground, an almost sure shot.

I shoot significantly more grouse each season than woodcock, and when I hunt with friends or relatives most either don't want to bother with woodcock or consider them simply the warm-up act for the real game—the ruffed grouse. Grouse are much spookier birds and harder to hit. They don't lie well for the dog most days, unlike woodcock, which will hold their ground until nearly stepped on. In fact, woodcock hunting without a dog is ineffective because they hold so tight. Hunting dogless or jump-shooting handicaps hunters since they will only kick up the birds they step on, and a decent dog increases the chance of finding woodcock twentyfold.

When flight birds migrate south, their numbers increase exponentially in good cover. It's then that they seem like gifts dropped from above, hence the term *fall of woodcock*. In times of heavy flight, it's possible to flush well over one hundred birds per day. On moonlit nights in late October and early November, we can hear their distinctive flight over the house, a whistling of wings sounding a bit like a mallard or wood duck. Once I saw one fly over a grocery store in Wausau and sit down in a small seep next to the parking lot. It's this abundance of birds, this fall of woodcock, that breeds contempt among hunters, the birds a dime a dozen.

On the last day of the woodcock season in what was essentially the last season for Gunnar, the first cover was bare and lifeless, with only whitewash to show that woodcock had used it. Earlier in the season, we had been through here and put up a dozen or so woodcock, but we were interested in grouse that day. Today we had come for the smaller bird, and after seeing the first cover empty I feared it had moved on and the dog would not live to smell and point another woodcock. It was a sobering thought on that gray day.

Despite the dog's age, we continued to the north and away from the car. I wanted to try one last spot. The cover looked nearly identical to the one we had just worked, and the ground was similarly covered with chalk, but this time the dog didn't even flash a point. Disappointed after half an hour or so, I turned the dog and started back toward the car, but he ignored me. He was working game, nose to the ground, slowing down like he was running out of battery power. A few more short steps and he eased into a point, not an elegant one like Ox's. Gunnar mostly stood his game, but he found birds. I walked in, and a bird exploded out of the cover to my right. It was a grouse, flying belt high through the popple. I waited until it flew above the dog's head and fired, and the bird magically crumpled. It was a hard shot, one I didn't expect to make, so the falling bird surprised me.

The dog was on the bird immediately. He picked it up then pranced around with it in his mouth, playing his game of keep-away and growling mischievously. The spring in his step, merriment in his eyes, and his wagging tail made me wish we could start all over again with Gunnar a blue-eyed puppy. I knew I shouldn't have let him hang on to the grouse, but as an old dog he was beyond redemption when it came to textbook retrieving. Besides, how many more chances would he get to do this, I thought? A few tooth marks in the meat didn't matter to me.

Finally I had to ask for the bird, not just once but several times. Gunnar released the bird, and I took it and smoothed back the wet breast feathers. The dog sat by my side and attempted to mouth the bird a few more times. We needed to get moving—I could sense the failing light, which comes early on a cloudy November day.

We stuck to logging roads on the way back, and the dog walked by my side, too tired to work the cover on either side of the road. He, too, seemed to want to be home. When we were within earshot of the road and I had begun to think about supper, Gunnar slowed then pointed. It surprised me, the dog right next to me on the logging road. I stopped and waited him out, but he remained rigid. To humor him I walked in for the flush. Up twittered a woodcock, which flew straight down the clearing made by the road through the woods. It was an easy straightaway shot, but I held my fire, wishing it well and hoping it would return again in the spring on its way north.

We continued on, and Gunnar moved ahead of me, excited by the scent and the flush. He loved to hunt woodcock. After a few moments, he stumbled and fell on his chin. He got up quickly and looked back at me as if I had tripped him. I prayed he would be around in the spring when the woodcock would return and drop in here like bread from heaven.

Things Unseen

APOINT IS LIKE A PRESENT—we never know what we are going to get until we unwrap it or, in the case of upland hunting, flush it. In the Wisconsin woods, I can be fairly certain a grouse or woodcock will emerge from my dogs' points. Sometimes I can tell, by the cover or the way the dog holds itself, whether or not the point will be a grouse or a woodcock. On rare occasions I can see a woodcock holding tightly mere feet, sometimes inches, in front of the pointing dog, trusting that its russet and earth tones will camouflage its presence. Without the dog I would never know it was holding there still as a stone.

In the field the dog is my link to the game. Without the dog I would be groping about the woods haphazardly, flushing birds by chance. Over the years I have learned to trust my dogs' noses, which is the sense they use to "see" the world, as they lead me around the cover. They use their eyes and ears, too, but mainly they are pulled around the woods by their noses, exploring an olfactory world we can only guess at. By integrating dogs into my hunting, using their instincts to sniff out and then point grouse and woodcock, we work together to capture game much more successfully than if we were hunting individually.

That written, the communication and teamwork between hunter and dog are never perfect. A few years back, in mid-November, I was hunting with my brother and Susan in Sawyer County. We had Ox out that day in a promising aspen cutting we had discovered the year before. This cover is small, perhaps one hundred acres, so it doesn't take long to work through, but it always seems to hold a bird or two. Shortly after we arrived, Ox was making game, his nose pulling him in the direction of promising scent. As he worked this thread, he started to slow. Some hunters liken this slowing to walking on eggshells or glass shards, but it seems to me as if the dog is running out of energy, like a wind-up toy, until he finally stops, literally in his tracks, and freezes into the point. When he freezes I get ready and remember the shotgun in my hands, hoping to hold up my end of the bargain.

"There it is," I said to the others. "Matt go left, Susan right." I directed them to either side of the point, but as I did so a black form rose up directly in front of Ox, and suddenly the picture was all wrong. He was pointing a black bear seven or eight yards away, moments before curled up and hibernating peacefully on a nest scooped out among the trees. The bear raised its bulky head and looked at us just like someone who had just been shaken awake in bed. I remember Susan crying, "What do we do? Shoot?" I bolted through the brush up to Ox, grabbed his collar and pulled him away from the bear and its intoxicating scent. One swat from that bear would have caved in Ox's head. Meanwhile the bear got up, stiff-legged, and wobbled away from us as Ox frantically tried to elude my grasp. The fool wanted a piece of that bear.

With a short lead, I tied Ox to a tree so he couldn't give chase, and we examined the nest, which looked like a massive bird's nest. On hands and knees, we smelled the still warm, withered grass lining. I had heard that bears reek, but the nest smelled like dry grass. While we took turns sniffing the nest on hands and knees, my brother and I both laughed at Susan and mimicked her, "What do we do? Shoot?" She defended herself and said she meant into the air, to scare off the bear. We returned a week later with a camera, thinking the bear had returned to its winter bed and expecting to take some pictures, but it was gone. Perhaps it had found a more apt place to hibernate.

So far that bear has been the most electrifying of my dogs' thousands of points. Well, maybe a skunk or two has zinged me a bit more—momentarily. Ox tangled with two porcupines before he realized his life was much better if he just pointed them. My dogs rarely get close enough to deer to point them, but they sure love to trail them until I call them off the scent. If they saw one, they would love nothing more than to give chase. Every hunting dog seems to think it's born to be a stag hound, or maybe the wolf in them can't resist the chase, and deer, with their white signal flag tail, seem more than willing to play the part of the fleeing prey.

Once in a while my dogs will point a turkey, and it always unnerves me when such a massive bird lumbers clucking out of thin grass—and thin air it seems. One would think you could see a ten-pound bird lying inches from your feet before it flushes, but their camouflage or the tense moment of the point hides them well. With our undeveloped sense of smell and eyesight more suited to looking across long savannas, we're in the dark as to what the dog has in front of his nose. Most of the time it's a game bird, however, my dogs obviously smelling the difference between a grouse and, say, a blue jay or the subtle disparity between a woodcock and a robin. They know what I want them to hunt, and do so most of the time, but every now and then they detour onto rabbit or deer scent, which makes perfect sense since both of those animals are game, and to a dog it probably makes a lot more sense to pursue rabbits or deer, which offer more meat. It's a wonder sometimes that they hunt birds for me at all.

In Iowa once while pheasant hunting, Ox pointed a Holstein calf in a ragweed patch, thinking he had a winner there. When it jumped up and lumbered out of the weeds and down the slough, Ox held staunchly, standing tall and waiting for me to fire. When the cow finally hobbled over the ridge of a picked cornfield bordering the ragweed strip, Ox looked back at me. Was he wondering why I didn't shoot, his latent wolf genes not understanding the fool with the gun? My Iowa in-laws didn't let me forget about that point for some time, reminding me several times that I had a mighty fine cow dog.

Black Friday

MID-NOVEMBER—ACCORDING TO the Wisconsin DNR General Deer Hunting Regulations, "It is illegal to possess any firearm in the field from 12:00 a.m. to 11:59 p.m. on November 21, 2008, unless the firearm is unloaded and encased within a carrying case." In other words, it's a crime to carry a gun of any kind in the woods before the opening day of the annual nine-day gun deer season. The DNR does make some isolated exceptions: target shooting at an established range, waterfowling, and hunting upland birds on a game preserve.

Simply put, the DNR does not trust anyone, including grouse hunters, with a gun in the woods on what I call Black Friday. According to our wildlife policy makers, the temptation to hold fire until Saturday is too great, what with all the gun deer season hype and the itchy trigger fingers that go along with the season. Unfortunately, a few bad apples might take a shot at a large buck or even a doe on Friday, then register the deer on Saturday. I'm also a deer hunter—a meat hunter who loves venison—and I understand the excitement, the shaking adrenalin rush as a deer enters the rifle sights, that provokes the DNR's ban.

Even so, it's hard for me to swallow this ban on all hunting on this day, often a perfectly good day to hunt birds. Wearing blaze orange, carrying a gun with #8 or #9 shot, and running a dog with a clanging bell strapped around its neck—that isn't exactly a textbook way to hunt deer. It rankles me that the DNR doesn't trust grouse hunters because of the crimes of a few poachers, making me feel like a kid in elementary school when the entire class is punished for the shenanigans of the class clown.

So while the majority of the hunters are celebrating the long-awaited opening day—a bigger deal than Christmas for many hunters in Wisconsin—for me Black Friday is the beginning of a dark period when we can't hunt grouse. Muzzleloader season follows the gun deer season, and then a four-day doe hunt follows, so effectively the gun deer season lasts over three weeks. In southern Wisconsin in the chronic wasting disease (CWD) zones, the gun deer season grinds on past Christmas and New Year's, the DNR thinking the longer season will cull more deer and eradicate the disease. It is a deadly disease that could decimate the herd so the DNR is rightfully worried about controlling its spread.

It is legal to hunt grouse during the Wisconsin gun deer season, but legal doesn't mean prudent. There's no way I would run my dogs in the woods during the gun deer season, for a few hunters are shot each year despite their conspicuous blaze orange clothing. If that's the case, how much easier to believe that a German shorthair, a Weimaraner, or even an English setter is a deer? I keep my dogs leashed when they are outside during the daylight hours lest they stray into somebody's sights. Hunters are accidentally shot; bullets ricochet off trees and brush and smash through houses and cars driving down the highway. A few Novembers ago, a young girl had just climbed into the backseat of a car to get a ride to school when a bullet blasted out the back window. Every year at least one hunter dies of a gunshot wound, and recently a colleague's son-in-law was shot and killed, devastating the family and leaving them numb with the tragedy.

My dogs never like this time of year as well, and they will go on chewing jags if not watched closely. Over the years they have chewed several gloves this week, as well as a couple pair of boots. By late November, they've hunted hard for two months, and suddenly, without warning, the hunting stops. They spend little time outside, just enough to do their business, and they can't understand why they are confined indoors so much.

Gun deer hunting is asymmetrical, barring many people from the woods, not just grouse hunters. Hikers, joggers, skiers, snowshoers, campers, and small game hunters enter the woods and fields at their own risk. Even as a deer hunter clad in blaze orange, I get nervous walking around the woods or to my stand. The DNR must know the effect the season has on nonhunters, but the economics and politics of gun deer hunting clearly influences the department. Gun deer hunting is big business, indirectly generating over a billion dollars a year; the Wisconsin DNR makes millions in gun deer license fees alone. Given the revenue generated, the pressure to cater to deer hunters is real.

We usually get out in the woods on Black Friday—one last time before the doldrums begin—gunless, of course. The woods are quiet, the calm before the storm to come at daybreak tomorrow. My hands empty, we ghost through the woods, my dogs hunting, oblivious of my lack of firearm or the coming layoff. We have had some memorable days on Black Friday. Once an eight-point buck chased a doe across the logging road we were walking and nearly ran over the dog. The dog stopped, tensed and ready to bolt, when he saw the doe cross twenty yards in front of his nose. He took a few jerky steps in her direction while I sharply barked a WHOA. Then the buck crashed out of the brush behind her and nearly bowled over the dog, which stood there shaking from excitement or fear.

On this day, however, we didn't get a big buck thrill. Instead we found a smaller and quieter one. Cresting a hill on a wide ski trail, Ox slid to his right, took a few tentative steps into the brush, then froze into a point. I walked toward him, but before I got there first one grouse and then two more bolted from the brush alongside the trail. Swinging my finger on the second one, which tilted to the right, I mouthed a *bang*. It set its wings and flew down into a heavily wooded depression, a frost pocket from the last ice age. Ox waited for the boom of my shotgun, but I only said, "Good dog. Good dog, Oxie."

Gun deer season—it's only nine days, I tell myself. The dogs, though, they never understand.

Narratives in the Snow

I T TOOK A MOMENT FOR THE IMAGE to register, but after a half dozen or so kicks and glides down the ski trail it did—WOLF. The large paw prints ran down the ski trail, each print larger than those of my eighty-five-pound dog, the rear tracks stepping into the front tracks in a long loping gait. Every so often the tracks stopped where the canine had investigated something along the edge of the trail, and they finally veered off to the northwest across a marsh and toward the tree line on the horizon. I, too, stopped and looked around, wondering if the wolf was somewhere in the brush watching me. For several minutes, I stood on my skis, my breath rising all around, and scanned the horizon. I wasn't afraid—it was more awe that there was something out there not quite comprehendible, something entirely wild and unpredictable.

We had received about an inch of snow overnight and into the early morning—a light, fluffy snow, the large crystals reflecting the sunlight in billions of prisms. With perfect tracking snow, I was skiing on what local cross-country skiers call the Swamp Loop, searching for tracks, grouse tracks actually. After a bit of snow, I make it a practice to go out and read the narratives written in the frozen crystals and, with this kind of snow, take an inventory of the birds and see how many made it through the dangerous fall and early winter. Back a ways, two grouse had skittered across the trail, but this wolf track was a much greater find.

I skied out of the swamp and up into the highlands, and about two kilometers later the wolf tracks reappeared on the trail. This time the tracks followed the ski trail for just a few hundred meters before turning back into the woods and the deeper snow there. Wolves, as well as other animals, use hard-packed trails, like a ski trail, since doing so is much more efficient than wallowing through a foot or so of softer snow in the woods.

Today in Wisconsin wolves are a fairly common sight, the state home to more than seven hundred animals in several dozen packs. The DNR estimates that in the 1960s less than five wolves still roamed Wisconsin. Nearly fifty years later, after making an improbable comeback, they range in just about every cover we hunt in northern Wisconsin. A few years back I tagged a deer in Clam Lake and talked about wolves with Adrian Wydeven, a Wisconsin DNR biologist who was registering deer at the convenience store there. As he checked my deer in, I asked him about a wolf sighting in the Nine Mile area in southern Marathon County. There was one wolf there, he said. I went through the inventory of the places we hunt—New Wood, Seeley, the Harrison Hills, the Willow—and he ticked off the packs roaming these areas. He wasn't telling me anything I hadn't already suspected. Their numbers and territory have been expanding for years, even down into the central part of the state where biologists figured they never would go.

Some hunters, particularly bear and deer hunters, fear and despise the wolf; a few have proclaimed they would have no problem shooting one on sight. During the 2008 gun deer season, six wolves were shot and killed. That bear hunters want to protect their dogs makes sense as wolves kill several bear hounds each year, and the DNR Web site lists these depredations, complete with maps warning hunters about the dangers of hunting around dog-killing packs. A bear hunter once showed me a grisly picture of a bear hound killed and devoured by wolves, and I had nightmares for several weeks afterward. In my dreams, though, it was a grizzly bear that killed my dog, and every time I buried him he would crawl out of the grave, a skeleton with strips of flesh hanging from him like old wallpaper. I have no idea how I would react—gun in hand—if wolves attacked my dog. I really don't want to find out.

Friends who deer hunt in Ontario each fall have described the sight of moose killed by wolves. One story they told was of a thirty-yard circle of trampled vegetation and scattered bones, a narrative written in blood. They said it looked like the struggle had taken days. A video circulating on the Internet, shot by a hunter in a tree stand, shows wolves taking down a cow moose. It was all I could do to keep watching the horror unfold on film. Wolves are not the cute dogs we iron onto sweatshirts sold in tourist towns, nor are they the tame creatures penned up in wildlife preserves. Wolves are deadly killers—that's their trade—and bear hunters know this side of their nature.

On the other hand, the fact that we have an expanding wolf population in Wisconsin gives me hope for all of the wild places we have left and optimism that we can maintain them. Wolves mean the state still has some big country left, unlike Iowa or Illinois, where the presence of the wolf doesn't seem possible. Nor does it seem like it would be tolerated. Wolves no longer need the unbroken tracts of wilderness biologists and hunters once thought they needed. A few years back the *Wausau Daily Herald* reported a pack skulking around the eastern side of Wausau very close to the city limits. Another breeding pair lives and works a large wetland territory halfway between Stevens Point and Wausau, in country once thought too small and tame to support them. Rumors fly around of packs in the most inconceivable places, but, unlike Bigfoot rumors, many of these stories have substance and credibility. We thought wolves could not live around or near densely populated areas or among rural areas of woodlots and farmland. We felt the social carrying capacity was significantly less than the biological carrying capacity. Regardless of what we think of them, the wolf has thrived, with and without our blessing.

I can count my number of wolf sightings on one hand and can still play back each of these sightings. I have heard them howling about the same number of times, the sound of wolves almost as impressive as the sight of one. It's a sound that has unhinged me every time, making my scalp tingle with an involuntary dread. Having heard the howls, I keep the dogs close to the cabin and in my sight for days until my dread evaporates. I value wolves, and maybe the idea of wolves even more so, but I fear for my dogs. I have witnessed dogfights, battles between ornery and hardheaded males who would fight to the death to be alpha, and they were unsettling. I can't imagine the terror of a wolf attacking one of my dogs, for either the dog or me, but it's a responsibility we must accept if we want to hunt in their territory. Wisconsin will be a poorer place indeed if we can't accept the wolf on its terms—tooth and claw—and we snuff out the narratives that every day they write across the landscape.

The Beauty of Clear-Cuts

THAT SURE LOOKS LIKE A GROUSE," I said. "Aren't those tail feathers hanging down?" Bob's golden retriever had just picked up an unidentifiable frozen hunk of bone and feathers. It was mid-January, and several of us were out snowshoeing with our dogs. "Nah, that's an organ. Bjorn's always finding gut piles," Bob said, thinking it was from a deer. We were cruising on snowshoes through county land north of our cabins where Bob often hunts.

Bob called to Bjorn, and he wheeled around with his prize. Sure enough—a grouse. "Good boy, Bjorn," Bob said, praising his dog for the retrieve. "You probably missed that one in October or November," I kidded, assuming the carcass was a bird. "He always finds the birds," Bob responded. I didn't think what he had in his mouth qualified as a bird. The breast and guts were gone, and it looked like the brains had been sucked out with a straw. Three gray tail feathers dangled from the chunk of frozen bone, skin, and feathers. Our non-hunting friend Scott suggested that a snowmobile had schmucked the bird, while Bjorn continued to parade around with his prize in his mouth.

We snowshoed over to the area where Bjorn had picked up the remains, and after a few minutes we found the story in the snow: blood, feathers, and the finely sculpted impressions of primary feathers sweeping the dry snow. It had all the marks of a goshawk or an owl dropping like a hammer from the sky and an unsuspecting grouse straying a bit too far into a clearing forty yards away from the edge cover and then the dense cover of the woods beyond that.

It looked like a brutal death, but Bjorn didn't make any analysis or judgment. Death was something he accepted by simply not thinking about it. Surviving in subzero temperatures wasn't much of bargain either, at least from our perspective, but the grouse in Bjorn's mouth was hardwired to survive even the depths of a brutal northern Wisconsin winter. It had survived the winter's cold and ice but not the goshawk.

The goshawk, *Accipiter gentilis*, feeds heavily on grouse, especially in winter. To a ruffed grouse, *Accipiter horribilis* would be more accurate. There's nothing gentle or genteel about the way a goshawk takes a grouse, which sits at the bottom of the winter food chain along with the snowshoe hare and the red squirrel. According to Gordon Gullion, the goshawk is the "most efficient" predator of ruffed grouse. When a goshawk spies a grouse, it is "probably seldom that the grouse survives," the hawk even pursuing ruffed grouse on foot through heavy cover. They do have difficulty pursuing a grouse flying through saplings, which is why aspen cuttings are so important to the grouse's survival.

In our day clear-cutting has received a lot of negative press, our image of a clear-cut a bombed-out mountainside once home to virgin Douglas fir. The media compares the cuttings to scars and wounds, even nuclear holocaust. A vast clear-cut can look like arrogance or folly. In fact, to some environmentalists clear-cuts are a metaphor for industrial society's rape of nature. It's true that Wisconsin, along with much of the other timbered areas of the country, was once razed with truly insolent effectiveness by timber barons and a culture with an insatiable appetite for wood, this heritage adding to our distaste for the technique of clear-cutting, but clear-cutting on a small scale is a much more benign process with valuable effects.

Small, properly managed clear-cuts (five acres or so) benefit ruffed grouse and woodcock, as well as other flora and fauna, which need the thriving and tangled riot of young growth that clear-cuts provide. The smaller cuts also create more edge cover than larger, industrial cuts, generating that in-between land where so many species overlap. Before chainsaws and skidders, fire once burned mature forest, creating natural "clear-cuts," essentially openings in which trees such as popple and brush such as dogwood and hazelnut can grow, but today for the most part we control forest fires so they won't threaten people and destroy their fixed property. Small clear-cuts can mimic these charred openings, and it's quite amazing how quickly these cuttings regenerate. Within five years they might hold woodcock, and soon the grouse follow, along with numerous other plants and animals. But these cuttings also benefit us, supplying much of the pulp wood that eventually becomes paper, and arguing against this technique on a printed page would be both hypocritical and ironic.

Before becoming addicted to grouse hunting, I used to think clear-cuts were unwise and ugly, scars on the landscape, and many still are, particularly those that stretch across the horizon or up a mountainside. Clear-cuts larger than five acres don't benefit grouse and other wildlife as much as smaller ones that provide plenty of edge cover, the transition zone between mature and immature trees. Large cuttings of forty acres or more aren't nearly as productive, except, of course, to loggers and the timber and paper industries. Not only ugly, they're difficult to walk through with the slashings strewn every which way clotting the ground while the new growth, at times, seems nearly impenetrable. A grouse hunter, though, once told me good cover tears your hat off your head, and so I continue to falter and bang my way through the tangle of young cuttings.

Grouse hunters understand the beauty of small clear-cuts, and on an October day when the aspen leaves have turned color, my eyes can pick out the patchwork gold of a clear-cut on a hillside from miles away. After the loggers have finished, the cuttings can look devastated, hideous and irresponsible, but shortly new growth takes over and these cuttings thrive and create a beauty all their own. It's an acquired taste for sure, and mine is biased by my grouse and woodcock hunting, but the beauty is there if one has the eye to see it.

Snow Walker

AN ATHABASKAN STORY SAYS THAT Ruffed Grouse taught the people how to weave snowshoes during a winter of big snow when the people were starving and couldn't travel around to hunt in the deep, soft snow. Ruffed Grouse didn't starve in the winter like people because he could get around and eat his favorite foods. Meandering around in the snowy woods, his telltale tracks looked as if he were out on a summer stroll.

The Athabaskans knew that in winter Ruffed Grouse grew hundreds of small appendages on his feet, which acted like the weaving on snowshoes and helped him float on top of the snow. Actually, modern research claims these appendages are more for gripping icy popple branches so grouse can feed on their favored buds than for floating on snow, but thinking of them as organic snowshoes makes a better story. Regardless, the increased surface area on their feet must help them some when they walk in powder.

Ruffed grouse, like all wild animals, don't have the option of going inside to warm up. They know nothing of forced-air heating systems or woodstoves radiating a life-giving warmth. Grouse live exposed in a beautiful yet brutal winter environment. Most never stray more than a couple of miles from their birthplace and therefore can't escape the harsh conditions of winter, and yet they actually thrive in this season.

Looking out an ice-frosted window of a heated and insulated house with the mercury below zero, I wonder how any creature can survive such a brutal climate. The chickadees at the feeder are suffering, especially with their small bodies, which quickly radiate whatever heat they can muster. Animals with large bodies, according to Bergmann's Rule, are more suited to northern climates because a larger body with relatively less surface area conserves heat. Karl Bergmann postulated in 1847 that animals would evolve larger bodies to retain heat in colder environments, but scientists now know that other adaptations for heat production and retention are more important than large bodies. Chickadees survive the cold by eating copious amounts of food and shivering the entire night in their sleep, the friction of their muscles keeping their bodies warm. Unlike grouse, they hunker down in the dense branches of a spruce or a balsam fir or find a hole in the tree bored by a pileated woodpecker. Knowing the conditions of their harsh lives, we don't complain about the rising costs of sunflower seeds and keep the feeder full.

Grouse, on the other hand, make the most of deep snow, using it for insulation, and this behavioral adaptation makes up for their relatively small bodies. They might fly headlong into deep snow, the way a high diver enters a pool. Or if the snow isn't quite deep enough to cover them completely, six inches or less, grouse will scrape snow around themselves with their wings. This is the least desirable option because it leaves them exposed to radiational cooling as well as predators. No matter how cold the ambient air temperature, which routinely drops to minus 30 degrees in northern Wisconsin, the temperature in a snow roost rarely drops below 20 degrees, the body heat of a grouse "warming" the snow roost. The coldest ambient temperature ever recorded in Wisconsin, minus 54, occurred two miles from my cabin in Seeley. This means a grouse roosting in snow could have been up to 75 degrees warmer than one roosting out in the open or huddled under a tree that brutal February night, perhaps the difference that night between life and death.

Below-zero cold snaps can be hard on grouse, as they are on any mammal trying to eke out an existence in northern Wisconsin. They must eat even more popple buds to fuel their furnaces, but above-freezing temperatures in winter, bringing thaws and perhaps even rain, might not be the blessing we think they are either. With a thaw or an ice storm, the snow crusts over, and grouse lose their snow roosts since they can't dig through the hard surface of the ice. Ice also coats their foods so thickly they can't get at them. If a cold snap arrives before deep snow falls, the birds must brave winter the best they know how—by eating as much as possible. With some snow on the ground, grouse will scrape out bowls in four to eight inches of snow, and if there's little or no snow they huddle in conifers or whatever shelter from the northwest wind they can find.

The colder the temperatures, the more grouse must eat, further exposing them to predators as they forage. Snow burrows are relatively safe, concealing ruffed grouse from not only avian but four-footed predators. My dogs rarely point snow-roosting grouse, whether due to the dryness of the winter air or the snow camouflaging their scent. They definitely can't see them in their little snow caves. Once a grouse burrowed into the snow in our backyard right off the path the dogs used everyday. Heading down the trail, one dog stopped a few feet from the burrow because he smelled something. While he was stopped, twitching his nose and looking puzzled or interested, not quite sure what he had there, the bird popped out of the burrow, almost between his front legs, showering him with snow. I ran into the house and grabbed my camera to get a picture of the snow cave. The bird's primary feathers at the end of its wingtips had sculpted the snow, lightly brushing the powder, but by the time I got back outside with the camera the dog had obliterated all traces of it. The dog had his nose deep in the snow roost, rooting around for a whiff of ruffed grouse.

Besides encircling their scent and keeping it from the sharp noses of canine predators, a snow burrow hides their brown or gray bodies from the sharp eyes of goshawks and great horned owls. Ruffed grouse feathers camouflage them for most of the year. Only in snow do their darker tones stand out, like Dorothy's ruby slippers in a black and white portion of *The Wizard of Oz*.

On occasion, I hunt grouse on snowshoes. In deep snow it's nearly impossible to pivot fast enough on snowshoes to get a shot off, so unless the bird flushes straight in front of a hunter on snowshoes it will live to see another cold day. Dogs have problems in the snow, too. They can't scent as well in the dry winter air. Ice collects between their toes, and transformed snow (thawed and refrozen) lacerates their paws. They labor in deep snow, too, jumping up and out of it or floundering along, and they tire easily, but the snow and cold rarely seem to dampen their enjoyment. I can't remember shooting a bird on snowshoes in the last ten years, but, like a dog, sometimes I just want to get out there.

I tried once to hunt grouse on cross-country skis, like a Tenth Mountain Division soldier or some sort of biathlete. Skiing out on groomed trails at a county forest where hunting is also legal, I kicked off my skis and set off on foot to hunt. This was a big mistake. My ski boots were cold and not really made for hiking in snow. Wearing them was like stomping around with buckets on my feet. Off the trails I floundered in the snow, which quickly worked its way up my pants, and soon I was wet to the knees. Snowshoes would have worked more effectively.

Once a deep snow falls and sticks on the ground, anywhere from mid-November until as late as after Christmas, I typically call it quits for the year, cleaning my shotgun one last time and storing my gear for another year. In 1991 two feet of snow fell on Halloween, and we didn't see bare ground until April. At Christmas I sometimes make an exception and hunt, a present for the dog, but in many years conditions are so poor—below zero or deep snow and sometimes both—I stay home and keep the wood burner humming. A dog in such weather is content to curl up on their pad next to the woodstove and hunt in the warm October of its dreams.

In Wisconsin the grouse season lasts until January 31 in the northern and central part of the state, where in total it's legal to hunt them for over four and a half months. Although I lack the science to back up my conviction, I think grouse should mostly be left alone in winter. The birds that have survived the dogs, the guns, the claws and teeth of other predators—they are the fittest of the species, surviving the natural selection of their harsh environment. They are seed birds for coming years, and we shouldn't subtract them from the gene pool. Besides, the goshawks and owls, the coyotes, and the occasional wolf deserve the meal more than a well-fed human like me does. Unlike us, grouse can't just drive to the grocery store and forage, nor do they have the technology to store foods for the starving time. They eat what they can find, and sometimes they're eaten, a meal for a hungry predator.

In winter I pray for deep snow, not only because I enjoy it but also for the sake of all the ruffed grouse trying to make it through to spring and another breeding season. Foraging for food, keeping warm, and avoiding hungry predators—their survival tiptoes across this razor's edge. In fact, I do a snow dance on occasion when we have been browned out and snow is scarce. If and when the snow falls and accumulates, the ruffed grouse, the snow walker, will use it to advantage—burrowing in it for warmth and scooting across the white crystals on its organic snowshoes.

The Last Day of the Season

THE SNOW LAY TWO FEET DEEP and we hadn't hunted in over a month. We were rusty, not having hunted much since the gun deer season in mid-November, but we had an itch to get out on this the last day of the season. I strapped on snowshoes, called Ox, and left the cabin, slogging through the powder down to a couple of likely spots.

Earlier in the year we had spooked a half dozen birds from one of these places, a deep pothole where aspen grow. We encountered no birds in the first cutting we worked through, not even the hint of a track in the snow. Deer tracks crisscrossed the snow, as did a pair of wolf tracks. The Seeley Highlands pack roams the area, and the wolves often cross to the southeast of our cabin. I stopped and examined the tracks until the dog came up and ran over the top of them.

After working the first spot, the snow was so taxing that instead of bushwhacking we cut down to a snowmobile trail and used the packed surface to get to the next place. We tried that at first, but after I fell twice in the deep snow, flailing about like a turtle on its shell, the snowmobile trail looked more appealing even if we did run into a sled or two. The second time I fell, it took me several minutes to right myself in all of the powder. It was as if I'd been caught in an avalanche, and I had to remove my snowshoes to get up. After finally getting back on my feet and cleaning the snow out of my gun barrels, we managed to get to the snowmobile trail and eventually struggle down into the pothole. We cut grouse tracks all over the cover but didn't flush a single bird. Ox didn't seem to mind, however. He was just glad to get out, stopping every so often to bite out the snow jammed in his paws. He was panting hard with all the effort but clearly on a lark and enjoying himself.

From the pothole cover, we continued north toward a ski trail, which we used to get back to our cabin. I'd had enough of the deep snow. My legs were cramping from lifting the snowshoes on my feet high enough to clear the snow on every step. Out on the trail, the dog once again dropped down on all fours and began chewing the ice out of his paws. I stopped to help him clear the ice so he could walk without pain. We made it back to the cabin twenty minutes later, birdless but happy, wrapping up another season.

Although the DNR regulations state that grouse season begins the third Saturday of September and ends on January 31 in the northern part of the state, the season really doesn't have clearly defined edges, not like the gun deer season, which runs just nine days. It doesn't have the opening-day hype of either the fishing season or the waterfowl season. It builds slowly through late September and doesn't hit full stride until October. We hunt the most from October until the beginning of the gun deer season. According to my journals,

I shoot over 80 percent of my birds in this six- or seven-week period, hunting only sporadically before and after this time. You could say the season starts and ends with a fizzle.

In September the heat, humidity, and heavy foliage limit my hunting. With a young dog that needs training and experience, we get out more, but less so with older, more seasoned dogs that don't need the experience. At the tag end of the season, snow cover limits my mobility and hunting. There have been years of little December snow, and we have hunted sporadically through the month. For a while I made a point of getting out around Christmas to try to shoot a bird for grouse pie on Christmas Day, our traditional dish. After a string of several bad, nearly snowless winters, the brown landscape and a longer season started to feel normal.

But the last few years have brought more snow. This past Christmas, we had more on the ground (eighteen to twenty inches) than we have had in a decade, Wausau receiving more snow in December of 2008 than in any previous month in our recorded climate history. Instead of going on my annual hunt on Christmas Eve or Christmas Day, I went cross-country skiing in the county forest. I made my way up a hill and over to a cutting that usually holds birds, and as I approached on the trail a grouse flushed. I stopped. Two more flushed. As I stood there, two more strutted on top of the snow, their ruffs up, before they flushed and disappeared in the winter twilight. I skied down the trail and around the cutting to a snowshoe trail running through the aspen. Since the snowshoe trail was well packed, I skied into the cutting on it, and reflushed another grouse. Grouse tracks led this way and that in the soft snow, and there was one deep divot where a bird had roosted, the tips of its wings brushing the snow where it fled its snowy bed.

As I stood there looking down at this delicate etching, a second grouse flushed from a nearby tree. Startled, I nearly slipped on the snow and only caught and rebalanced myself with a ski pole at the last moment. I couldn't help but laugh at myself for nearly pitching headlong into the snow.

I wished the bird luck as it flew deeper into the aspens. Soon, the grouse season officially over, it would only have to contend with tooth and claw predators for the rest of the winter. I prayed the bird would make it to spring and easier living.

Gunnar's Last Hunt

ABOUT TEN MINUTES DOWN THE TRAIL, tears started to pool in my eyes, building even as I tried to fight them back. I stopped, leaned my shotgun against a white pine, and tried to brush them away. I was raised in a stoic, Calvinistic family, where crying was the moral equivalent of not cleaning my plate or making my bed. My grandmother in her late eighties fell in her kitchen, broke her wrist, and lay on the floor for over twenty-four hours because she didn't want to call and bother anyone. With pain, we were taught to "just walk it off," not so easily done when the pain is emotional.

Eventually my eyes got so watery I sat down and leaned up against the pine next to my Browning. I couldn't have hit a grouse at that point anyway, aiming through tear-filled eyes. Ox, working the cover looking for birds, finally saw me sitting against the tree and loped back toward me, then sat shoulder-to-shoulder next to me. We had put down Gunnar the previous day, his cancer finally decimating him to the point where we could no longer avoid our responsibility, a decision we had been putting off for some time, pushing it back as I pushed against the tears. We wanted one more week, one more day, one more hour with Gunnar.

The next morning I needed to get out of the house, I needed movement, so I drove out with Ox to hunt in the same place where I shot Gunnar's first grouse some thirteen years before. The framed tail of the bird still hangs in our hallway. I thought a late October afternoon in the woods, where so many memories swirled, would comfort me. Perhaps, I thought, we would glimpse Gunnar flashing through the woods or hear the tinkle of his bell. He'd been gone about twenty-four hours, and the voice of denial told me he was only lost, and he would pop out of the woods and we could go on living as we had before. But he was gone, leaving his old pad by the wood-stove empty yet dented with the impression of his body. I wanted to wind the clock back and freeze it there, thoughts that didn't do me any good whatsoever, but I couldn't help but think them. My up-bringing scolded me for such self-indulgence, telling me he was "just a dog."

The previous month Gunnar did get to hunt one last time, his fourteenth season, a few miles from where Ox and I hunted that morning. I loaded Gunnar into the car, lifting in his withered body because he could no longer spring into the back, and drove to the county forest. After lifting him back out of the car, we set off down the trail. A few hundred yards down the trail, I almost turned around and called off our hunt. Gunnar would hobble ten yards, then squat and try to pee, the cancer making his bladder spasm, and he would look at me like he was saying, "I'm sorry." But shortly thereafter he got a whiff of scent and worked into the popple off the trail, beelining into the brush, scent pulled. He worked around for a few minutes, then eased into a point, his left front leg lifted. Had I known that was to be his last point, I would have broken down, but I didn't and simply waded in to flush the bird. It lifted off the ground between the thin popples in front of the dog and promptly vanished in the still green September aspen. Just like that, it was gone.

The scent of grouse revitalized Gunnar, however, and he worked the cover as though he'd been gifted a few years. We were only out for an hour or so, and I didn't get a shot, but that mattered little. We were doing what we loved to do and had done for the past thirteen autumns. After that hunt his condition worsened rapidly, and we never got out again.

A few months later, while cross-country skiing by the place where he had veered into the woods, I suddenly stopped, realizing where I was. I hadn't skied that loop with the intention of reliving that last hunt, some sort of sentimental journey, but I found myself there in the quiet of early winter by those bare aspen, a few crows cawing in the distance. And Gunnar was there, too, framed by the popple, his left paw raised.

After a few moments of leaning against the tree, I got up, wiped my eyes, grabbed my shotgun, and set off down the trail after Ox, who had moved on, impatient to be off. No sentimentalizing for him. Worn out by sorrow, I trailed off after my one living dog. A bit later I found Ox on a hard point, hemmed in by tag alders. He was facing me, so I figured he had the bird pinned between us. Circling instinctively to my left, I moved in. When the bird flushed a few of my steps later, it flew hard right at my head, then angled up sharply after spotting me. Pivoting to catch up with the bird, my gun caught in the brush, and by the time I'd ripped it out and faced the bird, it was nearly out of range and flying hard. Like a greenhorn, I ripped off two desperate shots, emptying both barrels, and the bird flew unfazed out of sight over tall red pines. I was bitterly disappointed, thinking some sort of Gunnar karma would mean all of the birds would fall to my gun on this day, that this would be a sign he was still with me. But that grouse flying hard over the pines killed that crazy notion.

For the rest of the afternoon, I stumbled through the motions of hunting. My hunting journal notes that Ox had four productive points, but I don't remember them—except the last one. That day my legs moved me down the trail, but my mind drifted back over several years. Gunnar had hunted this cover with me for fourteen seasons, so we had been through here at least a couple of dozen times in his lifetime. Many of those days and hunts I could see—grouse and woodcock pointed and flushed or the time we surprised a black bear dining on blueberries. Gunnar was young, strong, and healthy, flashing through the woods on happy feet.

When we were about a hundred yards from the car at the tail end of the hunt, Ox crossed the trail and worked from my left to my right, clearly on scent. My gun was broken open over my shoulder— I had given up for the day—so I dropped in two shells and quickly snapped it shut. Shortly he was on point. It didn't look like a likely place for a grouse—white pine and sparse brush—but I trusted Ox's hard point. Walking in, I wasn't surprised when a grouse whirred up. Just as my shotgun caught up to the bird and I was about to pull the trigger, it fluttered and landed in a low branch of the largest white pine. Lowering my shotgun, I couldn't help but laugh, as this scenario had often happened to Gunnar and treed birds unhinged him. He would bark madly, dancing around the tree like a circus dog, trying to figure out how he could climb it. On occasion, his barking had brought me to birds he'd treed, and I would try to hit them as they launched out of the tree, a shot that handcuffs many shooters.

As all this played through my head, the bird, ready to spring like a mousetrap, vaulted into the sky. Equally as wound up as the bird, I was primed, and it didn't get more than a few yards away from the tree before I fired. The grouse tumbled and dropped on Ox, who had no idea where the bird he'd pointed had gone. For all he knew, it had disappeared or I had missed, and then it magically fell out of the sky and glanced off his shoulder. Gunnar would have liked that. When I took the bird from Ox, I hugged him and then planted a kiss on the top of his black head. On that fine October day, he wasn't ready to follow after his buddy—and neither was I.

Counting in Dogs

I DON'T PLACE MUCH FAITH IN OMENS, but as we drove north to pick up our puppy and bring him home a grouse flushed across the road like a feathery rocket in front of our car. A brown-phased bird, it flew low across the highway, out of popples on the west side of the road and into balsam fir on the east side, their tops looking like the teeth of a crosscut saw set against the gray sky. It was a raw, cloudy April afternoon, crusty snow still lingering in the ditches and woods, although soon grouse would begin to drum and the woodcock would sing and dance in the clearings in what Aldo Leopold called the sky dance. Spring would come, and the birds would thrive.

We continued north through Park Falls, the self-titled Ruffed Grouse Capital of the World, where Alice's had replaced the old Ruffed Grouse Inn, although it, too, looked like it had fallen on hard times. Ox rode along with us in the car, sleeping most of the time but occasionally picking up his head for a look around. The previous hunting season he had contracted three diseases, two tick borne,

Lyme and anaplasmosis, as well as leptospirosis, bacteria he contracted most likely from drinking stagnant water in the field. His body wasted away daily before our eyes, his kidneys finally shutting down and laying him low. He would not live to see his thirteenth birthday and his twelfth hunting season, dying three weeks after we brought our puppy home. Fergus would not have the opportunity to learn from the old dog, to back a point on a woodcock, to learn how to course through the woods, to follow the big dog into cover Ox instinctively knew held birds. That apprenticeship was not to be.

As we drove home, Fergus asleep in Susan's lap and Ox sprawled out behind us in the station wagon, we talked quietly about the days when Gunnar and Ox were puppies. We were much younger then, living in a different house and just starting out in our professions. I had more hair, and we drove an old Chevy pick up. We now lived on the edge of town, although it was creeping closer every year. Houses now stand in the woods across the road, where woodcock once sang and danced.

A few days after we brought Fergus home and a few weeks before Ox died, I was outside in the front yard with Ox. He wandered over into the neighbor's yard, and their daughter, who was playing in the yard, asked me how old Ox was in "people years." I said he was almost thirteen. She tried to do the math in her head, struggling with a large number well beyond her years. Coming to her rescue, her mother said, "He's a lot older than Grandpa."

Walking back home with Ox plodding along at my side, I thought about people years and dog years. If Fergus lives to Ox's age,

I will be at least sixty years old, perhaps retired and with any luck still hunting. One more dog and I will be ready for Social Security. But just one dog ago it seemed we were young and lithe, just starting out in a life stretching ahead endlessly the way summer vacation does for schoolchildren at the end of May. That day, with Ox hobbling beside me, my life, measured in dogs, looked terribly short.

Bibliography

Bump, Gardiner, et al. *The Ruffed Grouse*. New York: New York
  Conservation Department, 1947.
Davis, Edmund Walstein. *Woodcock Shooting*. Belgrade, MT: Wilderness
  Adventures Press, 2000.
de la Valdene, Guy. *Making Game, an Essay on Woodcock*. Livingston, MT:
  Clark City Press, 1985.
Dizard, Jan. *Mortal Stakes*. Amherst: University of Massachusetts Press,
  2003.
Evans, George Bird. *The Upland Shooting Life*. New York: Knopf, 1971.
Fergus, Charles. *The Upland Equation*. New York: Lyons and Burford,
  1995.
Fergus, Jim. *A Hunter's Road*. New York: Henry Holt, 1992.
Ford, Corey. "The Road to Tinkhamtown." In *The Corey Ford Sporting
  Treasury*. Minocqua, WI: Willow Creek Press, 1987.
Foster, William Harnden. *New England Grouse Shooting*. New York:
  Scribner, 1970.
Gaddis, Mike. *Jenny Willow*. Guilford, CT: Lyons, 2002.
Grouse Tales. A bimonthly newsletter of the Loyal Order of Dedicated
  Grouse Hunters. Ridgeville, OH.

Gullion, Gordon. *Managing Woodlots for Fuel and Wildlife.* Coraopolis,
　PA: Ruffed Grouse Society, 1983.
―――. *The Ruffed Grouse.* Minocqua, WI: Northword, 1989.
Harrison, Jim. *Julip.* Boston: Houghton Mifflin, 1994.
Johnson, Don L. *Grouse and Woodcock, a Gunner's Guide.* Iola, WI:
　Krause, 1995.
Kellert, Stephen. *The Value of Life: Biodiversity and Human Life.*
　Washington, DC: Island, 1996.
Klinkenborg, Verlyn. "Our Vanishing Night." *National Geographic,*
　November 2008.
Knight, John Alden. *Ruffed Grouse.* New York: Knopf, 1947.
―――. *Woodcock.* New York: Knopf, 1944.
Leopold, Aldo. *For the Health of the Land.* Washington, DC: Island, 1999.
―――. *A Sand County Almanac.* New York: Ballantine, 1970.
London, Jack. *The Call of the Wild.* New York: Bantam, 1981.
Lundigran, Ted. *Grouse and Lesser Gods.* Camden, ME: Countrysport
　Press, 2002.
―――. *Hunting the Sun.* Traverse City, MI: Countrysport Press, 1997.
Matthiessen, Peter. *Wildlife in America.* New York: Viking, 1987.
Norris, Charles C. *Eastern Upland Shooting.* Traverse City, MI:
　Countrysport Press, 1989.
Ortega y Gasset, José. *Meditations on Hunting.* New York: Scribner, 1985.
Sheldon, William G. *The Book of the American Woodcock.* Amherst:
　University of Massachusetts Press, 1967.
Spiller, Burton. *Drummer in the Woods.* Mechanicsburg, PA: Stackpole,
　1980.
―――. *Grouse Feathers.* Lanham, MD: Derrydale Press, 1989.
―――. *Grouse Feathers Again.* Lanham, MD: Derrydale Press, 2000.
―――. *More Grouse Feathers, Again.* New York: Crown, 1972.
Strickland, Roy. *Common Sense Grouse and Woodcock Dog Training.* As told
　to John R. Rogers. Rockford, MI: Charles Main, 1981.

Thiel, Richard P. *The Timber Wolf in Wisconsin*. Madison: University of
  Wisconsin Press, 1993.
Thoreau, Henry David. *Walden*. Boston: Shambhala, 2004.
Turgenev, Ivan. *Sketches from a Hunter's Album*. London: Penguin, 1990.
Walrod, Dennis. *Grouse Hunter's Guide*. Mechanicsburg, PA: Stackpole,
  1985.
Wisconsin Department of Natural Resources. "Gray Wolf Distribution
  Map." 2009. http://dnr.wi.gov/org/land/er/mammals/wolf/
  wolf_map.htm.
Woolner, Frank. *The Complete Book of Woodcock Hunting*. New York:
  Lyons, 1974.
———. *Grouse Hunting Strategies*. New York: Lyons, 1970.